JUDAISM

THE BASICS

From the religion of ancient Israel to our own day, Judaism exhibits a history of much diversity and a tradition that goes back nearly 3,000 years. This book provides a simple and concise account of the religion, its narratives, beliefs, and practices as well as its secular history and importance within today's communities. Topics discussed include:

- Passover
- Rosh Hashanah
- Reform Judaism
- Scriptures
- Prayer
- Community

With a glossary of terms and extensive suggestions for further reading, *Judaism: The Basics* is an essential guide through the rich intricacies of Judaism, as a faith and as a culture.

Jacob Neusner is Research Professor of Theology at Bard College and Senior Fellow of the Institute of Advanced Theology at Bard. He is also a Member of the Institute for Advanced Study, Princeton NJ, and a Life Member of Clare Hall, Cambridge University, in England. He has published more than 900 books and unnumbered articles and is the most published humanities scholar in the world.

ALSO AVAILABLE FROM ROUTLEDGE

RELIGION: THE BASICS
MALORY NYE

FIFTY KEY CHRISTIAN THINKERS
PETER MCENHILL AND GEORGE NEWLANDS

FIFTY KEY JEWISH THINKERS
DAN COHN-SHERBOK

FIFTY KEY MEDIEVAL THINKERS
G. R. EVANS

THE ROUTLEDGE DICTIONARY OF JUDAISM
JACOB NEUSNER AND ALAN J. AVERY-PECK

GURDJIEFF: THE KEY CONCEPTS
SOPHIA WELLBELOVED

EASTERN PHILOSOPHY: KEY READINGS
OLIVER LEAMAN

KEY CONCEPTS IN EASTERN PHILOSOPHY
OLIVER LEAMAN

FIFTY EASTERN THINKERS
DIANÉ COLLINSON, KATHRYN PLANT AND ROBERT WILKINSON

WHO'S WHO IN CHRISTIANITY
LAVINIA COHN-SHERBOK

WHO'S WHO IN JEWISH HISTORY
JOAN COMAY, NEW EDITION REVISED BY LAVINIA COHN-SHERBOK

WHO'S WHO IN THE NEW TESTAMENT
RONALD BROWNRIGG

WHO'S WHO IN THE OLD TESTAMENT
JOAN COMAY

JUDAISM

THE BASICS

Jacob Neusner

Routledge
Taylor & Francis Group

LONDON AND NEW YORK

First published 2006
by Routledge
2 Park Square, Milton Park, Abingdon, Oxon OX14 4RN

Simultaneously published in the USA and Canada
by Routledge
270 Madison Ave, New York, NY 10016

Routledge is an imprint of the Taylor & Francis Group, an informa business

Typeset in Aldus Roman and Scala Sans by
Taylor & Francis Books
Printed and bound in Great Britain by
TJ International Ltd, Padstow, Cornwall

British Library Cataloguing in Publication Data
A catalogue record for this book is available from the British Library

Library of Congress Cataloging-in Publication Data
Neusner, Jacob, 1932-
  Judaism: the basics / Jacob Neusner.
    p. cm.
  Includes bibliographical references and index.
  ISBN 0-415-40175-5 (hardback : alk. paper) -- ISBN 0-415-40176-3 (pbk. : alk. paper) 1. Judaism. I.
Title.

BM562.N49 2006
296--dc22

2006007312

ISBN10: 0-415-40175-5   ISBN13: 978-0-415-40175-3 (hbk)
ISBN10: 0-415-40176-3   ISBN13: 978-0-415-40176-0 (pbk)
ISBN10: 0-203-08876-X   ISBN13: 978-0-203-08776-0 (ebk)

CONTENTS

PREFACE

This book provides a simple and concise account of the basics of the religion Judaism, its narratives, beliefs, practices, contemporary expressions, as well as its secular history and a glimpse into its vital present. Here Judaism speaks in its own voices through its classical writings and contemporary representatives.

How are we to identify what is basic in such a complex religious tradition? Answering that question is not easy, because Judaism has had a long history, from the religion of ancient Israel set forth in the Hebrew Scriptures (Christianity's "Old Testament") to our own day. It is a history that exhibits much diversity, but the norms of conviction and conduct, which permit us to speak of "Judaism" and not just varieties of Judaism or "Judaisms," do make themselves known. These are four.

First, from ancient times to the present day, the same sacred calendar of Sabbaths and festivals and holy time has governed in nearly all communities of Judaism. All keep the Sabbath day, though each has its own rules of what is permitted and prohibited on the holy day. All celebrate Passover, "the season of our freedom," celebrating the Exodus from Egypt. All observe Rosh Hashanah, the New Year, and Yom Kippur, the Day of Atonement. What is basic to Judaism, then, is a universal calendar, a single mode of celebration of holy time.

Second, told for all time and touching hearts through the ages, specific narratives such as we meet in Chapters 1 through 5 convey the meaning of those and other celebrations and common convictions, and these stories have persisted as well. The narratives explored here come from canonical documents on which most modern and contemporary communities of Judaism, including Reform, Conservative, and all of Orthodoxy, draw heavily.

Third, all varieties of Judaism affirm the centrality of the Hebrew Scriptures of Ancient Israel, the Torah broadly construed, which Christianity knows as "the Old Testament." No community of Judaism ignores Scripture, though all join debate on the authority and meaning of the ancient writings. But the debate does not extend to whether or not the Scriptures are relevant; all concur that they are. They possess a voice everywhere, a veto only in particular settings.

Fourth, all communities of Judaism affirm the unity of God or "monotheism," though each sets forth that conception in its own way. In the prayers that synagogue communities recite, we find the outlines of a common theology. Judaism possesses a universally acknowledged creed, subject to many interpretations, to be sure.

This fourth matter requires explanation. A universal set of prayers, as much as a universal calendar, has governed Judaic worship from antiquity to the present time. Most, though not all, communities of Judaism follow a single pattern of prayer, involving the recitation of a creed. "Hear, Israel, the Lord our God, the Lord is one," forms the creedal center of all Judaic worship, morning and night, Sabbath, festival, and everyday. No community of Judaism omits it, though each has its interpretation of its meaning. And that shared creed covers no trivial matter. "Hear, Israel," states the message of monotheism that forms the center of all Judaic worship. It is a matter to which we shall return in due course in Chapter 7.

So much for the basics of Judaism, covering all versions of that complex of religious traditions. What about the state of public opinion among Jews when the books say do or believe one thing, and some of the people do or believe another – or do or believe nothing of the kind? Some Jews actively identify with the Jewish ethnic group but are atheists. That fact requires us to distinguish the ethnic group from the religious community. The definition and fate of Judaism as a religion are not the same as the definition and fate of the Jews as an ethnic group. For, as I shall spell out in the Introduction, the Jews as an ethnic group encompass secular, ethnic *Jewishness* as well as religious, theological *Judaism*.

Ethnic Jewishness encompasses matters of culture and sensibility, history and literature, a strong sense of forming a community of fate, if not one of faith. Theological Judaism adds to the ethnic program a religious worldview and way of life formed in Scripture and tradition. As a matter of fact, persons who qualify as Jews by ethnic origin (birth to a Jewish mother) include some who practice a religion other than Judaism. And, conversely, gentiles too enter the community of Judaism through religious conversion (circumcision of males, immersion of males and females), thereby forming part of the ethnic group as well.

When in these pages we identify the basics of Judaism, the religion, we ask those that practice the faith and find guidance in the holy books to show us what they mean by Judaism. We do not take account of ethnic preferences of Jews who do not affirm the authority and teachings of the holy books, who do not believe in God for example.

The upshot is simple. A book – a set of religious ideas – divorced from a social group is not Judaism. A book by itself may speak about Judaism but does not embody Judaism. And a social group of Jews who dismiss as merely interesting the holy books of Judaism does not represent Judaism either. The accumulation of opinions on any given subject of every individual Jew also does not add up to Judaism. Only a community of Judaism with its consensus does.

To embody Judaism therefore are required the testimony of the holy books and the adherence of faithful practitioners of their teaching. The great British theological scholar, Raphael Loewe, offers the distinction between the (ethnic) Jew and the (religious) Judaist. All Judaists by definition belong to the ethnic group, the Jewish people. But not all members of the ethnic group are Judaists.

In Chapters 1 through 5 we shall put that distinction to work. There we shall define Judaism by examining rituals and associated myths that are nearly universally practiced among people who, by their own word, are not only ethnic Jews but religious Judaists. Then Chapters 6 and 7 rely on the holy books to define what is basic in Judaism, its law and theology. Chapters 8, 9, and 10 describe the historical origins and the medieval and modern continuation of basic, classical Judaism. These trace the secular histories of the varieties of Judaism.

Chapter 11 then explores a single issue paramount in the now and for the future of all contemporary versions of Judaism: How Judaism may speak about the Holocaust and the State of Israel. We conclude with examples of theology pointing toward the future of authentic Judaic expression. These cases drawn from contemporary theological journalism, Orthodox and Reform, will indicate how the Torah will speak to the twenty-first century when communities of Judaism, from Orthodox to Reform, concur on everything important and nothing trivial.

I mean to address any literate person with a clear account of basic Judaism. If I have come near attaining that goal, I owe it to my wife, Suzanne Richter Neusner, who read the book in its first draft, and my editor, Andrea Hartill, who guided writing the second. Both worked hard and I appreciate their effort.

Jacob Neusner

ACKNOWLEDGMENTS

Biblical passages follow the translation of the Revised Standard Version: Herbert G. May and Bruce M. Metzger (eds) (1965) *Oxford Annotated Bible with the Apocrypha: Revised Standard Version*. New York: Oxford University Press and are used by permission. Translations of rabbinic texts are my own. Translations of liturgical passages were prepared by me in consultation with the various presentations of the Siddur and Mahzor, the standard prayerbooks of Judaism, by Jules Harlow (ed.) and published by The Rabbinical Assembly, New York, copyright by The Rabbinical Assembly. These are identified where they occur.

The essays by Professor Lawrence Hoffman and Rabbi Avi Shafran reproduced in Chapter 11 derive from the *New York Jewish Week* and are subject to copyright. They are reproduced with the permission of the authors and the *New York Jewish Week*.

Thanks go to all mentioned above.

INTRODUCTION

Defining Judaism

Some people view religions as personal and private. One cannot study what is private, however, only report about it. But religions in a worldly setting form communities of the faithful. They are public, shared, and there to be studied in the setting of society. Religious communities form cultural systems with an ethos or a way of life, an ethics or worldview, and a theory of the origin and character of the community or an ethnos. The religious system holds together because each of its parts answers questions about the purpose of that community and its calling.

RELIGION AS A CULTURAL SYSTEM: ETHOS, ETHICS, ETHNOS

Judaism is a religion like any other. In this-worldly, social perspective, any religion (or religious tradition) forms a cultural system that is comprised by three components, (1) its worldview, (2) its way of life, and (3) its definition of the community of the faithful. "Ethos" refers to the worldview, "ethics" to its way of life and definition of virtue, and "ethnos" to the social entity ("community," "church," "holy people") that takes shape among the believers.

What then marks as religious such a system of the social order? It is the system's stress on God's concern for the group that marks the system as religious and not secular. The introduction of the dimension of the divine is what distinguishes a religious from a secular system of the social order and its culture. Theology, thus, is to a religious system of the social order what ideology is to a secular one.

That definition of religion as public and communal serves especially well when we come to Judaism, which frames its entire message in the setting of the life of a group that calls itself "Israel." In religious context this refers (as we shall see in Chapter 1) to those who take personally Scripture's stories. Abraham, Isaac, and Jacob are the ancestors and models of Israel.

"Israel" in the holy books of Judaism is made up of those who see themselves in a direct lineage from the children of Abraham, Isaac, and Jacob and heirs of those that received the Torah at Mount Sinai (all matters to which we shall return presently). Those that tell about themselves and their group, today, those tales of long-ago times and far-off places that the Torah sets forth comprise "Israel" in Judaism.

JUDAISM: THE SOCIAL ENTITY, ITS WAY OF LIFE AND WORLDVIEW

What if we wanted to identify a Judaic religious community? What are the components we should look for, the data to be collected, organized, and interpreted? The basic elements of Judaism, the religion, are defined in these specific terms:

Social group / Israel? The first requirement is to find a group of Jews who see themselves as the embodiment or representative of the "Israel," to which Scripture's stories refer. Israel, that is, the Jewish People, forms the family and children of Scripture's Abraham, Isaac, Jacob, Sarah, Rebecca, Leah, and Rachel, the founding fathers and mothers. That group will regard the narratives of Scripture as speaking about them. So an "Israel" is comprised by a group of Jews (children of a Jewish mother or converts to Judaism) who take personally, as the account of who they are and of their group's origins and meaning, the story told by the Scripture (the Torah). (Reform and Reconstructionist Judaism refers to a Jewish father or a Jewish mother.)

Worldview / Torah? The second requirement is to identify the forms through which that distinct group expresses its worldview. Ordinarily, we find that expression in writing, so we turn to the authoritative holy books that the group studies and deems God-given, that is, the group's Torah or statement of God's revelation to Israel.

Way of life / commandments (Hebrew: *mitzvah, mitzvoth* (pl.))? A group expresses its worldview in many concrete ways, through music (singing the Torah and the prayers, for example), dance (parading with the Torah in worship), drama, rite and ritual; through art and symbol; through politics and through the ongoing institutions of society; through where it lives, what it eats, what it wears, what language it speaks. The group also makes its statement through the opposites of all these: What it will not eat, where it will not live, whom it will not accept for marriage. Synagogue architecture and art bear powerful visible messages. The life cycle, from birth through death, the definition of time and the rhythm of the day, the week, the month and the year – all of these testify to the worldview and the way of life of the social group that, all together, all at once, constitute a Judaic religious system. The group itself will call its system "Judaism" pure and simple.

WHAT QUESTION DOES JUDAISM ASK AND WHAT ANSWER DOES IT SET FORTH?

How does religion work and what holds the whole together? A religious system – way of life, worldview, theory of the social entity that lives by the one and believes in the other – identifies an urgent and chronic question facing a given social group. The system in each of its elements answers that question, and the answers cohere. So the system holds together through a pervasive question that finds a self-evidently valid answer.

That urgent question may be posed by the political situation of that group. Consider, for instance, the story that the Jews tell themselves about their history. Scripture speaks of Israel's building a house for God in Jerusalem, which was destroyed in 586 B.C.E. History, furthermore, records the rebuilding of that Temple and the destruction of the Temple a second time, in 70 C.E. So the Israel of Judaism, which aspires to be holy to God, finds itself in the status of a defeated minority. Jews from antiquity onward formed their theory of the group, "Israel," and its way of life and worldview around the theme of exile from the Holy Land and return to the Holy Land, explaining the situation of defeat by appeal to the pattern of exile and return.

Repeating its answer to that urgent question – How have God's people come to such a state? – in context of countless details, the system says the same thing about many things. So it provides an answer that for the faithful is self-evidently valid and everywhere transparent.

But what happens when new questions arise to which the received system presents no answers? When the urgent question loses its urgency, the religious system faces competition from other Judaic systems that do ask acutely relevant questions. An example from our own day suffices to show what is meant. As we shall see in Chapter 11, the Holocaust represents the advent of such a shift, as the received systems adapt to the new crisis or give way to new systems that will respond to the crisis.

In the case of the Jews as a social group, for example, one urgent question that such a small, dissenting community, living as a minority in various political and cultural majority-settings and adapting itself to the life of the majority, must answer is, "Why be different?" Judaism, through its narrative, transforms difference into destiny. It explains just why that "Israel" of which it speaks must preserve its unique way of life and worldview to realize God's purposes.

That is the power of the Judaic telling of the story set forth in Scripture: It is the capacity to answer, in small details, again and again, the urgent question facing the Jews as a group wherever over time and space they have found themselves, that is, why the group persists and should continue to do so. The story, repeated endlessly, explains God's plan and expectation for the Israel, the tale of which the Torah tells.

JUDAISM AND THE JEWS

What does make the definition of Judaism uncertain is the confusion of Judaism as a religious tradition with opinions held by Jews, an ethnic group or nationality (depending on the context). That confusion leads to the identification of popular opinions held among Jews with the dogmas of the religious tradition of Judaism.

Why is that an error? First, it omits reference to the authoritative statements of Judaism in its holy books or in the name of its holy sages. But a religious tradition is not something made up as you go along. Second, not all Jews are religious at all. Some do not believe in God. They define themselves as an ethnic group or nationality deriving from a common history and secular culture or, in the State of Israel, as a nationality – but not as a religious community sharing a way of life and a worldview. Their atheism does not change their status as part of the Jewish people viewed as a secular, social entity, a "people," an ethnic group, a nationality, even as a nation-state. But it does deny them the authority to define Judaism, the religion. And secular Jews cannot deny the existence of the religion, Judaism.

Defining Judaism as "the religion of the Jewish People" treats the religion Judaism as "what the Jews believe." The state of opinion among Jews then forms the criterion of not just Jewish (ethnic) public opinion but Judaic (religious) doctrine. Two problems follow. First, authoritative teachings of holy books, including the prayer book, while affirmed by faithful practitioners of Judaism, conflict with popular opinion held by numbers of ethnic Jews. For example, in law and liturgy is the belief in the Resurrection of the Dead. God is blessed in the three-times-a-day Prayer, "You give life to the dead through great mercy ... blessed are you, who keeps faith with those that lie in the dust." Denial of the origin, in the Torah, of that teaching deprives the non-believer of a portion in the world to come (Mishnah-tractate Sanhedrin 10:1). But a survey of Jewish opinion will produce only a minority of the total Jewish population that maintains that belief, though a majority of Jews that practice

Judaism does. The Resurrection of the Dead will concern us in Chapter 7 and again in Chapter 11.

Second, all communities of Judaism affirm the unity of God. God is understood as the creator of Heaven and Earth, who revealed the Torah to Moses at Sinai, and who will redeem Israel, the Holy People, at the end of history. These form parts of the standard creed. But a significant sector of the Jewish group does not believe in God in any terms. More generally, a fair proportion of the Jewish population rejects religiosity (whether Judaic, whether generic) in favor of secular humanism, and a smaller but still formidable proportion of the Jews practice some religion other than Judaism, Buddhism or a sect of Christianity, for example. Yet those that reject belief in the Resurrection of the Dead and those that view being Jewish ("Jewishness") as an ethnic, not a religious ("Judaic") affiliation regard themselves, and are regarded by others, as valid Jews.

With what outcome? If by Judaism is meant "the religion of the Jewish People," then the consequent ethnic account of Judaism forms both a religion and an ethnicity. It both believes in God and is atheistic, both comes to expression in holy books and accommodates every opinion and its opposite – whatever the state of the holder's knowledge and piety. We cannot define what is basic to Judaism if we confuse the religious community of Judaism with the ethnic group, the Jewish People. That confusion yields Judaism as the sum total of the opinions held by individual Jews – a mass of confusion and contradiction. The way toward defining basics of Judaism requires distinguishing secular Jews, who practice no religion, from religious Jews, who practice a form of Judaism. The former, as we noted in the Preface, we call simply "Jews," and the latter, "Judaists," that is, that sector of the Jews that practices Judaism.

So, stated simply: All Judaists – those who practice the religion, Judaism – also are Jews, but not all Jews are Judaists. That is to say, all those who practice the religion, Judaism, by the definition of Judaism fall into the ethnic group, the Jews, but not all members of the ethnic group, the Jews, practice Judaism. When we ask about basics of Judaism, then, we speak only of Judaists in the setting of how Judaism transforms and enchants the everyday life.

What about the alleged ethnicity of Judaism? Judaism is not an ethnic religion, for it accepts converts by an act of faith. Nor are the

Jews a people of a single religion, for Jews practice Buddhism and Christianity but remain within the ethnic lineage. But a religion also is more than its creed, expressed through liturgy, and we cannot regard the faith as a set of abstract ideas divorced from the life of the people who refer to those ideas. What happens to the Jews as an ethnic group or to the State of Israel as the concern of the Jewish people wherever they are located shapes issues facing Judaism, the religion. The Holocaust was a demographic catastrophe for the Jewish people and also defined the principal theological dilemma facing Judaism in the twentieth century and beyond. The demographics of the Jewish people – decline in population in particular – make an impact on the life of the synagogue. So we cannot draw too rigid a distinction between the ethnic and the religious in the context of the Jewish people and Judaism. The ethnic group and the religion reciprocally shape the life of one another. Chapters 10 and 11 illustrate how that is so.

But we shall shape an ideal type: A normative, essential, basic Judaism for Chapters 1 through 7 that is defined by the holy books and the liturgy paramount in time. Then, in Chapters 8 through 10 we shall take account of variations produced by modern and contemporary times in the definition and practice of Judaism, inclusive of Zionism, also with its complicating factor of secular and religious formulations. In Chapter 11 when we come to contemporary Judaism, we shall deconstruct our ideal-type and treat Jewishness and Judaism as an amalgamation. That amalgamation prepares the reader to make sense of the facts of Judaism and Jewishness likely to be encountered in ordinary life.

THE ISRAELITE PEOPLE, THE ISRAELI STATE

A word at the outset is required to clarify a further source of confusion on basics, the multiple meanings of the word "Israel."

By "Israel" with its adjective "Israelite" before 1948, the theological and legal writings of Judaism meant, "the unique, holy community" of Judaism, the Jewish people wherever located, the Israel of which Scripture speaks. That same "Israel" of Scripture finds representation in the here and the now by the Jewish people. For millennia, the Holy People called "Israel" had yielded the adjective, "Israelite," a member of the community of Judaism. "Israel" did not refer to a nation-state or to a nationality. "Israelite" was synonymous with Jew or with "Hebrew," after the main language of Scripture.

When Zionism, or Jewish nationalism, reached its realization and the Jewish state came into being in 1948 in what Judaism knows as the Land of Israel, calling the Jewish state "Israel" or "the State of Israel" created a second meaning for the category "Israel," now a place people go to, a citizenship people adopt, a nation-state. That political "Israel" yielded the adjective "Israeli."

Now, if all Jews are not Judaists, so too all Israelites are not Israelis. And, as a matter of fact, not all Israelis are Israelites; a fifth of the population of the country is Muslim or Christian. The upshot, basic to the study of Judaism, is simply put: The Psalmist's "He that keeps Israel does not slumber or sleep" refers to the Jewish people, and, a great many Jews believe, it refers also to the Jewish State.

In these pages, by "Israel," without further qualification, the holy and unique people of Judaism is meant, and where the *State of Israel*, a location to which people go, comes under discussion, it is called "the State of Israel" and is carefully distinguished from Israel, the Jewish people, scattered throughout the world, sharing in a variety of nationalities.

PART I

JUDAISM THROUGH STORY

1

DEFINING JUDAISM
THROUGH STORIES

To define Judaism out of its own liturgy and law, in this and the next four chapters we examine stories Judaists (practitioners of Judaism) tell themselves when they celebrate great occasions. These are the stories that convey the theological convictions of Judaism. Each occasion contains within itself a story that defines a principal part of Judaism for nearly all Judaists. That narrative explains their way of life. It speaks through symbols to convey their worldview. It tells them their group's history and defines their destiny. It links present to past to future. Above all, a rite basic to all communities of Judaism, past and present, defines the group, the community of Judaism, spelling out who is the "Israel" of which a given version of Judaism speaks.

Religions are best defined through the stories that they tell to account for concrete facts of the here and now. For through narratives that touch the heart rather than through abstract formulations of theological propositions religions make their impact on the faithful.

To practice Judaism, therefore, means to act out in behavior and belief the key stories that are told in the Torah, the Hebrew word for Instruction, referring specifically to the instruction set forth by God to Israel at Mount Sinai. Judaism stakes its claim to knowledge of God upon that Instruction.

Take, for instance, the story that carries the theological message, God made the world. The narrative in Genesis 1–3 of what God *did and does* in creating the world rather than the proposition that God *is* creator of the world best conveys Judaism's medium for stating its convictions about God as creator of all things. So, too, when it comes to defining the community of Judaism, we identify the story universally told to answer that question: Among all the nations and peoples of the world, who is an Israelite and what is Israel? We shall meet the story in Chapter 2. In the tales that answer that question, "Israel" forms an extended family, in line with the stories of Genesis about Abraham, Isaac, and Jacob, or by "Israel" are meant those who, assembled at Mount Sinai, accepted the Torah revealed by God to Moses, in line with the stories of Exodus. And the nations, or gentiles, are defined as well through the same stories.

That preference for the concrete narrative evidence leads to the question, how shall we know *which* narratives to examine as critical to Judaism? Scripture presents many candidates. But Judaism selects only a few of them. These it repeats in endless variations. The criterion is simple. Judaism defines its worldview in the stories it chooses for the celebration of great occasions in the sacred calendar, Sabbaths and festivals for example. The creation of the world, the Exodus from Egypt, the giving of the Torah – these are primary stories repeated on the great occasions of the sacred calendar.

So too events in the life cycle, birth and marriage, for instance, find their place within narratives of Israel's history, the tale of the prophet Elijah figuring at the rite of circumcision eight days after birth, the creation of Adam and Eve and the promise to restore the Temple in Jerusalem playing a critical role in the marriage rite, as we shall see in a later chapter.

Then what will signal the greatness of the occasion? Events of weight in the life of the community mark occasions to be situated within the biblical record. We turn to the narratives of Passover (Chapter 3), which celebrates the Exodus from Egypt; the Days of Awe (New Year and Day of Atonement), which emphasize the binding of Isaac at Genesis 22 (Chapter 4); and the rites of marriage and circumcision (Chapter 5), thus the stories that account for the life of the community as a whole. These basic stories place into context the rites of passage of the individual Israelite.

SCRIPTURE AND THE NARRATIVE REPERTOIRE OF JUDAISM

Since Judaism selects chapters of Scripture's narratives and amplifies them in the setting of its way of life, we begin with Scripture. By "Scripture," which Christianity knows as "the Old Testament," in Judaism is meant, the privileged collection of books that all together Judaism calls "the Torah," or Teaching. "The Torah" bears a variety of reference points, beginning with the Pentateuch, the Five Books of Moses, which are Genesis, Exodus, Leviticus, Numbers and Deuteronomy. But "the Torah" may also encompass the whole of the Israelite Scriptures. And in due course, the teachings of the great rabbinic sages would be classified as teachings of the Torah.

For Judaism, the Torah or Teaching sets forth the master narrative of the human condition. It is God's story of who "we" (humanity, Israel) are. The Torah begins with creation and the advent of Adam and Eve and traces the history of humanity to the formation of Israel, the people who accepted the Torah and God's rule in it. Judaism holds that in the Torah God's perspective upon the story of humanity prevails. Judaism turns Scripture's stories into rules. It transforms them into examples that form a pattern. How a Judaic narrative bears the theological message of Judaism is illustrated in the story of Abraham and the idols in Box 1.1.

WHICH BOOKS OF SCRIPTURE TELL THE STORY? THE TORAH AND THE FORMER PROPHETS

Judaism may, therefore, be defined as "the religion of the Torah revealed by God to Moses at Mount Sinai." And that formulation carries us to the question, of what precisely does this revealed Torah consist? The Hebrew Scriptures are divided into three components: The Torah proper, which to begin with refers to the five books of Moses, then the prophets, and finally the writings. The Hebrew is *Torah, Nebi'im* (prophets), *Ketubim* (writings), and it yields T / N / K, or TaNaK. Box 1.2 contains the contents of Scripture.

Let us rapidly consider the specific scriptural books that, read as a continuous, unfolding account, tell the story that Judaism acts out.

BOX 1.1

Here is an example of how Judaism defines its theology through storytelling. The point is the representation of Abraham as the first monotheist. How his reason and critical mind led him to monotheism takes the form of the narrative at hand.

GENESIS RABBAH XXXVIII:XIII

A. "Haran died in the presence of his father Terah in the land of his birth, in Ur of the Chaldeans" (Gen. 11:28).

B. Said R. Hiyya [in explanation of how Haran died in his father's presence], "Terah was an idol-manufacturer. Once he went off on a trip and put Abraham in charge of the store. Someone would come in and want to buy an idol. He would say to him, 'How old are you?'

C. "He said, 'Fifty years old.'

D. "He said, 'Woe to that man, who is fifty years old and is going to bow down to something a day old.' So the man would be ashamed and go his way.

E. "One time a woman came in with a bowl of flour, and said to him, 'Take this and offer it before them.'

F. "He went and took a stick, broke the idols, and put the stick in the hand of the biggest idol.

G. "When his father came back, he said to you, 'Why in the world have you been doing these things?'

H. "He said to him, 'How can I hide it from you? One time a woman came in with a bowl of flour, and said to me, "Take this and offer it before them." Then this idol said, "I'll eat first," and that idol said, "I'll eat first." One of them, the largest, got up and grabbed the stick and broke the others.'

I. "[Terah] said to him, 'Why are you making fun of me! Do those idols know anything [that such a thing could possibly happen]? [Obviously not!]'

J. "He said to him, 'And should your ears not hear what your mouth is saying?' He took him and handed him over to Nimrod.

K. "He said to him, 'Bow down to the fire.'

L. "He said to him, 'We really should bow down to water, which puts out fire.'

M. "He said to him, 'Bow down to water.'

N. "He said to him, 'We really should bow down to the clouds, which bear the water.'

O. "He said to him, 'Then let's bow down to the clouds.'

P. "He said to him, 'We really should bow down to the wind, which disperses the clouds.'

Q. "He said to him, 'Then let's bow down to the wind.'

R. "He said to him, 'We really should bow down to human beings, who can stand up to the wind.'

S. "He said to him, 'You're just playing word-games with me. Let's bow down to the fire. So now, look, I am going to throw you into the fire, and let your God whom you worship come and save you from the fire.'

T. "Now Haran was standing there undecided. He said, 'What's the choice? If Abram wins, I'll say I'm on Abram's side, and if Nimrod wins, I'll say I'm on Nimrod's side. [So how can I lose?]'

U. "When Abram went down into the burning furnace and was saved, Nimrod said to him, 'On whose side are you?'

V. "He said to him, 'Abram's.'

W. "They took him and threw him into the fire, and his guts burned up and came out, and he died in the presence of his father.

X. "That is in line with the verse of Scripture: 'And Haran died in the presence of his father, Terah' (Gen. 11:28)."

THE TORAH PROPER: GENESIS, EXODUS, LEVITICUS, NUMBERS, DEUTERONOMY

The first book of the Torah / five books of Moses is Genesis, the story of creation and the formation of the holy family, Abraham and Sarah, Isaac and Rebecca, Jacob and Leah and Rachel, yielding the children of

BOX 1.2

> Torah: The five books of Moses cover the beginnings of the people of Israel as sojourners in the Land and as slaves in the land of Egypt freed by God through Moses and led by him to the border of the Land.
>
> Prophets: Then the former prophets, Joshua, Judges, Samuel, and Kings, tell the story of how Israel got the Land and lost it, but would get it back. The latter prophets, Isaiah, Jeremiah, Ezekiel, and the Twelve Minor Prophets, go over the same ground. These are Hosea, Joel, Amos, Obadiah, Jonah, Micah, Nahum, Habakkuk, Zephaniah, Haggai, Zechariah, and Malachi.
>
> The writings: These are comprised by a diverse set of writings: Psalms and Prophets, Job, Song of Songs, Ruth, Lamentations, Ecclesiastes (Hebrew: Qoheleth), Esther, Daniel, Ezra, Nehemiah, and Chronicles.

Jacob, also called Israel, thus the children of Israel, an extended family beginning with Abraham and Sarah. It ends with the children of Jacob / Israel going down to Egypt, to sojourn there in a time of famine in the Land that God had given to Abraham and Sarah and their descendants. The second book of the Torah, Exodus, tells how the Egyptians enslaved the Israelites, but how God heard their cry and sent Moses, the prophet, to gather them out of Egypt and lead them back to the Land. Moses led the Israelites through the wilderness of Sinai to Mount Sinai, where God gave him the Torah. The third book of the Torah, Leviticus, records the laws of the sacrificial service that God afforded to Israel as a means of atonement for sin, covering the priesthood that would preside over the offerings. The fourth book of the Torah, Numbers, tells the story of Israel's forty years of wandering in the wilderness, prevented from entering the Land. The fifth book of the Torah, Deuteronomy, retells the story of Israel in its redemption from Egyptian slavery and its wandering in the wilderness, ending with the vision of Moses for Israel's future in the Land.

JOSHUA, JUDGES, SAMUEL, AND KINGS

The prophets are divided into the former prophets and the latter prophets. The scriptural books of Joshua, Judges, Samuel, and Kings are the former prophets. Isaiah, Jeremiah, Ezekiel, and the twelve minor (because of the brevity of the writings) prophets – Hosea, Joel, Amos, Obadiah, Jonah, Micah, Nahum, Habakkuk, Zephaniah, Haggai, Zechariah, and Malachi are the latter prophets.

THE FORMER PROPHETS

The principal prophetic writings, Joshua through Kings, tell the story of Israel in the Land of Israel, from the conquest and settlement led by Joshua, through the progressive decline of Israel in the Land by reason of its disloyalty to God and its "straying after false gods." First, the people asked for a monarch to replace the prophetic rulership of judges divinely inspired, the last of whom was Samuel. The result was King Saul, replaced by King David, and succeeded by King Solomon. Then, after the united monarchy of Saul, David, and Solomon, the people broke into northern and southern wings, Israel on the north, Judea on the south.

Scripture represents the fate of the two kingdoms as God's response to the faithlessness of the people. They were found wanting. The Assyrians in 701 B.C.E. consequently conquered the northern kingdom, called Israel, and the ten tribes that comprised (northern) Israel were taken into exile, never to return. The southern kingdom, made up of the tribes of Judah and Benjamin and called Judea, centered around Jerusalem and its temple. Judea persisted for another century but then was conquered in 586 B.C.E. by the Babylonians, who inherited the Assyrian Empire and who destroyed the temple on Mount Zion in Jerusalem and exiled the Judeans to Babylonia. When in 538 B.C.E. the Persians in turn conquered the Babylonians, however, the Judeans were allowed to return to Zion, and some did. Led by Ezra, the scribe, and Nehemiah, the viceroy of the Persians, in 450 B.C.E. they rebuilt the temple and restored its offerings and proclaimed the Torah of Moses to be the foundation document of restored Israel in the Land of Israel and everywhere else Jews lived. So much for what is called "the authorized history," which emerges from a continuous reading of Genesis–Exodus–Leviticus–Numbers–Deuteronomy, followed by Joshua–Judges–Samuel–Kings as interpreted by Isaiah, Jeremiah, Ezekiel, and the minor prophets. How Judaism transformed this narrative into the foundations of its way of life and worldview remains to be seen.

THE LATTER PROPHETS: ISAIAH, JEREMIAH, EZEKIEL, AND THE TWELVE MINOR PROPHETS

Who were these prophets? The book of Isaiah contains prophecies that pertain to several periods, the first thirty-nine chapters focusing on the events that culminated in 701 in the conquest by the Assyrians of the northern kingdom, but their failure to pursue the siege of Jerusalem; the next group, Chapters 40–56, address the period of the return to Zion in the sixth century B.C.E.

The book of Jeremiah focuses upon the final decades of the southern kingdom, from about 620 to 586. The prophet both warns the Judeans to submit to Babylonia and, at the time of the siege, also prophesies the ultimate restoration of Israel to its land. From the perspective of the Babylonian exile the book of Ezekiel addresses the same period.

THE WRITINGS

The writings are Psalms, Proverbs, Job, the books of Daniel, Ezra, Nehemiah, and Chronicles, and the five scrolls, which are as follows: Song of Songs, Ruth, Lamentations, Ecclesiastes (Hebrew: Qoheleth), Esther. These writings are diverse and do not fit as a group into that continuous, authorized history of how Israel got, lost, and was restored to the Land. Of the group, Chronicles recapitulates the stories of Samuel and Kings, and Ezra and Nehemiah tell about the return to Zion under Persian suzerainty. Job, Qoheleth, and Proverbs are rich in moral reflection and wisdom.

So, at the foundations of Scripture's many stories in the Torah and the prophets, Genesis through Kings, Judaism identifies a single pattern, a governing motif: The pattern of exile and return, meaning, possession and loss of the Land and recovery of the Land as well. And, finding in Genesis 1–3 the story of humanity in the persons of Adam and Eve, Judaism compares the experience of Adam and Eve and the experience of Israel, drawing the lessons common to them both.

FROM THE HISTORY OF ANCIENT ISRAEL TO A NARRATIVE OF THE HUMAN CONDITION

And where, among the Torah, prophets, and writings, do we find the stories for the great occasions of which we spoke just now? If the Torah sets forth the master narrative of the human condition, what tale does it tell? The first two of these parts of Scripture, the Torah meaning the five books of Moses and the prophets, Joshua, Judges, Samuel and Kings, as we just saw, tell a continuous story. It concerns the formation of the Holy People, Israel, and its covenant with God. This covenant explains how Israel got the Land of Israel, how it lost the Land of Israel, how it recovered the Land of Israel, and how, by adhering to the imperatives of the Torah, it could continue to possess the Land. Scripture tells, then, the story of Israel and the Holy Land: Its possession of the Land and the conditions for its continued settlement there, its loss of the Land, and the beginnings of its recovery thereof.

Given the formidable volume, diversity, and complexity of the books of Genesis through Kings, we must ask how the diverse stories, for instance concerning creation, the Exodus, the loss of the Land and the recovery of the Land, are turned into a systematic and coherent account of Israel? How are the prophets' admonitions and revelations in God's name transformed into a cogent and concrete theological message? What vision of the whole imparts to the details of Scripture's many laws the cogency of a legal structure and system?

The answer derives from the rabbinic sages of the Torah – the founders of Judaism as we know it – who flourished in the first six centuries of the common era. In their systematic reading of Scripture, they turned Scripture's cases and narratives into a system of rules. They established the norms of Judaism. We shall now see the rabbis' basic point and how it is formulated out of the facts of Scripture. Here is how they discern the patterns that the narratives yield and define the meanings of those patterns.

ADAM, EVE AND EDEN, ISRAEL AND THE LAND

The rabbinic sages compare the story of Israel's possession and loss of the Land with the story of Creation and Adam's and Eve's possession and loss of Eden. The key is their quest for patterns, and in Scripture they find a huge pattern. It is one that shows the parallel between Adam and Eve's possession and loss of Eden by reason of disobedience and Israel's possession of the Land of Israel and loss of the Land by reason of disobedience. From the rabbis' perspective, the entire narrative of Scripture from Genesis through Kings shows how Israel in the Land recapitulates the story of Adam and Eve in Eden. But it is a pattern with a difference. Adam and Eve lost Paradise, never to return. Israel went into exile but atoned for its sin and then got back to the Land, and, with the Torah for guidance, would endure there.

In this reading, the books of Genesis through Kings tell a simple story, first, the prologue that sets forth the human condition, Genesis 1–11, on how Adam and Eve were given Paradise but sinned and brought pain, suffering, and death to the world; then how God tried again, ten generations later, with Noah. All humanity descends from Noah, who survived the flood that wiped out everybody else. Ten generations after Noah came, in Abraham and Sarah, the beginnings of a humanity worthy of being designated "in our image, after our likeness," that is, humanity in the model of God. Then, from Genesis 12 through the end of the book of Kings, the story shows how Israel, like Adam, was given Eden, now the Land of Israel, but lost it, like Adam, through sin in the form of rebellion against God's will. But here comes the difference between Adam, without the Torah, and Israel, with the Torah: While Israel, like Adam, sinned and lost the Land, Israel also breaks out of the pattern. Guided by the Torah, Israel would atone for its sin. Then it could recover and now hold the land by loyalty to God's will expressed in the Torah.

The rabbinic sages thus took Scripture to form not a one-time narrative but a model and a pattern, in the theory that – in the case of the book of Genesis, for example – the deeds of the founding generations, Abraham and Sarah, Isaac and Rebecca, Jacob and Leah and Rachel, define a paradigm for their descendants. So they went in quest of the patterns implicit in the narratives.

ADAM AND ISRAEL: THE PARALLEL STORIES

Now to the centerpiece of the sages' reading of Scripture. In the case at hand, the rabbis found intelligible markers in parallel details of two stories, Adam's and Israel's. And everything follows from that discovery. Whatever happened to Adam happened to Israel. Then as Adam represented all humanity, so Israel represents all humanity, with the difference represented by the Torah.

The text before us derives from Genesis Rabbah, the reading of the book of Genesis by the rabbinic sages in *c.* 450 of the common era. Seeking patterns in abundant data like natural historians in a tropical forest, the rabbinic sages constantly cite verses of Scripture to provide the facts at hand. The sages discern out of those facts the patterns and regularities that signal the workings of laws, just as in natural history the philosopher turns the facts of nature into natural laws. The rabbis construct with those verses a pattern that permits the comparison they have in mind.

The method is clear. Notice how various books of Scripture, both the Torah and the prophets and the writings, contribute to the exposition. Scripture is now turned into a vast corpus of freestanding facts, and the task of the faithful sage is to move from case to law.

GENESIS RABBAH XIX:IX.1–2

> A.   R. Abbahu in the name of R. Yosé bar Haninah: "It is written, 'But they [Israel] are like a man [Adam], they have transgressed the covenant'" (Hos. 6:7).
>
> B.   "'They are like a man,' specifically, like the first man. [We shall now compare the story of the first man in Eden with the story of Israel in its land.]"

The sage, Abbahu, cites Hosea 6:7, which compares Israel to Adam, and says that both Israel and Adam have violated the covenant that they had with God. Now the sage identifies God's action in regard to Adam with a counterpart action in regard to Israel, in each case matching verse for verse, beginning with Eden and Adam. Adam is brought to Eden as Israel is brought to the Land, with comparable outcomes:

C. "'In the case of the first man, I brought him into the garden of Eden, I commanded him, he violated my commandment, I judged him to be sent away and driven out, but I mourned for him, saying "How ..."' [which begins the book of Lamentations, hence stands for a lament, but which, as we just saw, also is written with the consonants that also yield, "Where are you"].

The task of the sage is to tell what happened between God and Adam and to back up that account with proofs deriving from verses of Scripture, taken as facts. So he will go over the list of transactions – brought him into the Garden, commanded him, and so on – and adduce verses of Scripture that show that God had done just that.

D. "'I brought him into the Garden of Eden,' as it is written, 'And the Lord God took the man and put him into the garden of Eden'" (Gen. 2:15).
E. "'I commanded him,' as it is written, 'And the Lord God commanded ...'" (Gen. 2:16).
F. "'And he violated my commandment,' as it is written, 'Did you eat from the tree concerning which I commanded you?'" (Gen. 3:11).
G. "'I judged him to be sent away,' as it is written, 'And the Lord God sent him from the garden of Eden'" (Gen. 3:23).
H. "And I judged him to be driven out ... And he drove out the man" (Gen. 3:24).
I. "But I mourned for him, saying, 'How ...' ... And he said to him, 'Where are you?','" (Gen. 3:9), and the word for 'where are you' is written [with the letters that produce the word], 'How ...'"

Now that the exegete has proved the case for Adam, he turns to Adam's descendants, who are Israel. God went through the same transaction with Israel and the Land of Israel as with Adam and Eden. Now comes the systematic comparison of Adam and Eden with Israel and the Land of Israel:

J.   "So too in the case of his descendants, [God
     continues to speak,] I brought them [Israel] into the
     Land of Israel, I commanded them, they violated
     my commandment, I judged them to be sent out
     and driven away but I mourned for them, saying,
     'How ...'"

K.   "I brought them into the Land of Israel ... And I
     brought you into the land of Carmel" (Jer. 2:7).

L.   "I commanded them ... And you, command the
     children of Israel" (Exod. 27:20). "Command the chil-
     dren of Israel" (Lev. 24:2).

M.   "They violated my commandment ... And all Israel
     have violated your Torah" (Dan. 9:11).

N.   "I judged them to be sent out ... Send them away,
     out of my sight and let them go forth" (Jer. 15:1).

O.   "And driven away ... From my house I shall drive
     them" (Hos. 9:15).

P.   "But I mourned for them, saying, 'How ... '"... How
     has the city sat solitary, that was full of people"
     (Lam. 1:1).

We end with a citation of the opening sentence of Scripture's book
of Lamentations, the writing of mourning produced after the destruction of the Temple in Jerusalem in 586 B.C.E. by the Babylonians.
Here we end where we began: Israel in exile from the Land, like
Adam in exile from Eden. But the Torah is clear that there is a
difference: Israel can repent. So the destruction of the Temple and
the alienation of Israel from God are deemed comparable with the
loss of Eden and the alienation of Adam from God. Israel stands for
all humanity.

These persons, Israel and Adam, form not individual and particular one-time characters in historical time, but exemplary
categories. Adam stands for humanity without the Torah. Israel is
Adam's counterpart, Israel is the other model for humankind,
possessing, and possessed by, the Torah.

Adam's failure defined Israel's task, marked the occasion for the
formation of Israel. Israel came into existence in the aftermath of
the failure of Creation with the fall of humankind and their ultimate near-extinction; in the restoration that followed the Flood,

God identified Abraham to found in the Land, the new Eden, to realize his will in creating the world.

Israel, above all, embodies God's home in humanity, his resting place on Earth. I hardly need repeat the point I made in the Introduction, that this definition of "Israel" cannot be confused with any secular meanings attributed to the same word, for example, nation or ethnic entity, counterpart to other nations or ethnic groups.

2

WHO AND WHAT IS ISRAEL?

Scripture's stories concern Israelites not only in biblical days but throughout history. The "Israel" of which Judaism speaks lives in an eternal present tense, in which past, present, and future coincide. The great occasions of Israel's past mark the present as well. Judaists take for granted that Scripture speaks of them, its narratives tell their story. Scripture's narrative is taken for granted as history, and the facts of that history – God's promises to Abraham, God's covenant at Sinai with Israel – prove propositions of theology in an eternal present. Scripture accounts for the present in the past and points toward the future in the present.

SUPPLYING THE SUSTAINING SCRIPT

Judaism calls the faithful "Israel," and calls upon Scripture's stories to answer the question of what and who Israel is. The answer is an extended family, a covenanted people to God through the Torah. Scripture supplies narratives that answer that question. These stories do not record one-time, past-tense history. They do more than commemorate and call old times to mind. Rather, they set forth enduring patterns, lessons and laws that apply everywhere and always. They portray the perpetual present. That is why Israelites tell the stories of biblical Israel but find themselves in those tales. The rabbinic sages thus find verses of Scripture awaiting application to their own times.

What that means is best illustrated in a story about when the Messiah will come. The key question that troubles Israelites in the picture that Judaism presents is what will become of Israel, meaning, when will the Messiah gather the Israelites together in the Land of Israel and restore them to their intended position. They scoured the prophets in particular, seeking information on what is to come about and when. Here is how in the narrative Judaism accords to the Israelites command of their own destiny. The story involves the meeting of the prophet Isaiah, called "our rabbi," "our lord," and Israelites in quest of hope. The passage begins with a citation of Isaiah 21:11 that asks the question, "Watchman, what of the night?"

YERUSHALMI TAANIT 1:1

II.5

    G.   "[The oracle concerning Dumah]. One is calling to me from Seir, 'Watchman, what of the night? Watchman, what of the night?' (Is. 21:11). The Israelites said to Isaiah, 'O our Rabbi, Isaiah, What will come for us out of this night?'"

    H.   He said to them, "Wait for me, until I can present the question."

    I.   Once he had asked the question, he came back to them.

Isaiah goes to God to inquire, and comes back with the answer, found in the very next verse of the book of Isaiah: "Morning comes, and also the night. ... "

    J.   They said to him, "Watchman, what of the night? What did the Guardian of the ages say [a play on 'of the night' and 'say']?"

K. He said to them, "The watchman says: 'Morning comes; and also the night. [If you will inquire, inquire; come back again]'" (Is. 21:12).
L. They said to him, "Also the night?"

Isaiah's message, "morning ... also night ... " puzzles the Israelites, who await a message of hope. In that context, how can he speak of morning and night?

M. He said to them, "It is not what you are thinking. But there will be morning for the righteous, and night for the wicked, morning for Israel, and night for idolaters."

Now the message of the Watchman is clear: Morning for the righteous, night for the wicked; morning for Israel, night for idolatry. And that raises the obvious next question: When?

N. They said to him, "When?"
O. He said to them, "Whenever you want, He too wants [it to be] – if you want it, He wants it."

Israel is responsible for its own condition. When the Israelites want the morning, it will come. But what obstacles now prevent it?

P. They said to him, "What is standing in the way?"
Q. He said to them, "Repentance: 'come back again'" (Is. 21:12).

Israel must repent its sin and God will forgive them, a message of sublime hope, which underscores Israel's command of its own sorry situation. The story ends with a concrete lesson: What is to be done?

R. R. Aha in the name of R. Tanhum b. R. Hiyya, "If Israel repents for one day, forthwith the son of David will come."

S.   "What is the scriptural basis? 'O that today you
would hearken to his voice!'" (Ps. 95:7).

The first lesson is general: If Israel repents for a single day, the
Messiah, son of David, will come. What is that single day? As we
shall see in Chapter 6, when we meet the Ten Commandments, the
Sabbath is that single day. If all Israel keeps a single Sabbath, they
will repeat the situation that prevailed in the creation of the world,
when God completed creation and found it very good and sanctified
it with Sabbath rest.

How have the rabbinic sages recast Scripture into theology in
the form of a story, a conversation? This account of how Israel's
own conduct dictates its future invokes a variety of narratives. It
begins with the stories of creation and the Sabbath as the mark of
perfection and sanctification. Israel in the wilderness, depending on
God's succor for its daily food, forms yet another chapter of the
story. Past, present, and future meet in its allusions. The condition
of Israel, a defeated nation, finds its explanation in the people's
conduct. What is required for the restoration to Paradise is repentance. Israel can bring about the advent of the Messiah through
repentance and repose on the Sabbath – those two actions make all
the difference.

The stories that register take for granted theological definitions
and propositions and simply allude to them. Judaism presupposes
for its stories a set of abstract rules or laws, and it takes for granted
in presenting those rules the stories that give the rules concrete
reality: Isaiah's message from the Watchman in the story just now
examined. What repentance requires is spelled out in the exposition
of the Day of Atonement, which shows us how law and legend join
together to form a complete statement.

MISHNAH-TRACTATE YOMA 8:9

A.   He who says, "I shall sin and repent, sin and
repent" –

B.   They give him no chance to do repentance.

C.   [If he said,] "I will sin and the Day of Atonement will
atone," – the Day of Atonement does not atone.

    D.   For transgressions done between man and the Omnipresent, the Day of Atonement atones.

    E.   For transgressions between man and man, the Day of Atonement atones, only if the man will regain the good will of his friend.

    F.   This exegesis did R. Eleazar b. Azariah state: "'From all your sins shall you be clean before the Lord' (Lev. 16:30) – for transgressions between man and the Omnipresent does the Day of Atonement atone. For transgressions between man and his fellow, the Day of Atonement atones, only if the man will regain the good will of his friend."

    G.   Said R. Aqiba, "Happy are you, O Israel. Before whom are you made clean, and who makes you clean? It is your Father who is in heaven,

    H.   "as it says, 'And I will sprinkle clean water on you, and you will be clean' (Ezek. 36:25).

    I.   "And it says, 'O Lord, the hope [*miqweh*, immersion pool] of Israel' (Jer. 17:13) – Just as the immersion pool cleans the unclean, so the Holy One, blessed be he, cleans Israel."

Preemptive atonement is ruled out. Repentance and atonement – regret for sin, resolve to straighten out, repair the damage done by sin so far as that is possible – represent in abstract terms the concrete message of the prior story. That is, the Messiah will come when Israel (1) repents and (2) observes Sabbath repose – those two things. Israel has that power to repent that conciliates God to restore Eden on the Sabbath day.

ISRAEL AND THE NATIONS

What story does Judaism tell to answer the question, who and what is Israel? The answer is a tale that shows how the gentiles reject God, whom they could and should have known in the Torah. They refused to accept the Torah, and all else followed. The proposition then moves in these simple steps:

1. Israel differs from the gentiles because Israel possesses the Torah and the gentiles do not.
2. Because they do not possess the Torah, the gentiles also worship idols instead of God.
3. Therefore, God rejects the gentiles and identifies with Israel.

And where do considerations of justice and fairness enter in? The same justice that governs Israel and endows Israel with the Torah dictates the fate of the gentiles and denies them the Torah. And, predictably, that demonstration must further underscore the justice of the condition of the gentiles: "measure for measure" must play itself out especially here.

The gentiles deprived themselves of the Torah because they rejected it, and, showing the precision of justice, they rejected the Torah because the Torah deprived them of the very practices or traits that they deemed characteristic of and essential to their being. That circularity marks the tale of how things were to begin with, but in fact describes how things always are; it is not historical but philosophical. The gentiles' own character, their nature, the shape of their conscience, then, now, and always, accounts for their condition – which, by an act of will, they can change.

What they did not want, that of which they were by their own word unworthy, is denied them. And what they do want condemns them. So when each nation comes under judgment for rejecting the Torah, the indictment of each is spoken out of its own mouth, its own self-indictment then forms the core of the matter. Given what we know about the definition of Israel as those destined to live and the gentile as those not, we cannot find surprising that the entire account is set in that age to come to which the gentiles are denied entry.

When they protest the injustice of the decision that takes effect just then, they are shown the workings of the moral order, as the following story that conveys the governing pattern explains:

BAVLI TRACTATE ABODAH ZARAH 1:1 I.2/2A–B

A. R. Hanina bar Pappa, and some say, R. Simlai, gave the following exposition [of the verse, "They that fashion a graven image are all of them vanity, and

their delectable things shall not profit, and their
own witnesses see not nor know" (Isa. 44:9)]:

B.   "In the age to come the Holy One, blessed be He,
will bring a scroll of the Torah and hold it in his
bosom and say, 'Let him who has kept himself
busy with it come and take his reward.' Then all the
gentiles will crowd together: 'All of the nations are
gathered together' (Isa. 43:9). The Holy One,
blessed be He, will say to them, 'Do not crowd
together before me in a mob. But let each nation
enter together with [2B] its scribes, and let the
peoples be gathered together' (Isa. 43:9), and the
word 'people' means 'Kingdom': 'and one
Kingdom shall be stronger than the other' (Gen.
25:23)."

We note that the players are the principal participants in world
history: The Romans first and foremost, then the Persians, the
other world rulers of the age:

C.   "The Kingdom of Rome comes in first." ...
H.   "The Holy One, blessed be He, will say to them,
'How have you defined your chief occupation?'
I.   "They will say before him, 'Lord of the world, a vast
number of marketplaces have we set up, a vast
number of bathhouses we have made, a vast
amount of silver and gold have we accumulated.
And all of these things we have done only in behalf
of Israel, so that they may define as their chief
occupation the study of the Torah.'
J.   "The Holy One, blessed be He, will say to them,
'You complete idiots! Whatever you have done has
been for your own convenience. You have set up a
vast number of marketplaces to be sure, but that
was so as to set up whorehouses in them. The bathhouses were for your own pleasure. Silver and gold
belong to me anyhow: "Mine is the silver and mine
is the gold, says the Lord of hosts" (Hag. 2:8). Are
there any among you who have been telling of

> "this," and "this" is only the Torah: "And this is the
> Torah that Moses set before the children of Israel'
> (Deut. 4:44)." So they will make their exit, humiliated.

The claim of Rome – to support Israel in Torah study – is rejected
on grounds that the Romans did not exhibit the right attitude,
always a dynamic force in the theology. Then the other world rule
enters in with its claim:

> K.   "When the Kingdom of Rome has made its exit, the
>   Kingdom of Persia enters afterward."
> M.   "The Holy One, blessed be He, will say to them,
>   'How have you defined your chief occupation?'
> N.   "They will say before him, 'Lord of the world, we
>   have thrown up a vast number of bridges, we have
>   conquered a vast number of towns, we have made
>   a vast number of wars, and all of them we did only
>   for Israel, so that they may define as their chief
>   occupation the study of the Torah.'
> O.   "The Holy One, blessed be He, will say to them,
>   'Whatever you have done has been for your own
>   convenience. You have thrown up a vast number of
>   bridges, to collect tolls, you have conquered a vast
>   number of towns, to collect the corvée, and, as to
>   making a vast number of wars, I am the one who
>   makes wars: "The Lord is a man of war" (Exod.
>   19:17). Are there any among you who have been
>   telling of "this," and "this" is only the Torah: "And
>   this is the Torah that Moses set before the children
>   of Israel' (Deut. 4:44)." So they will make their exit,
>   humiliated.
> R.   "And so it will go with each and every nation."

Rome and Iran stand as the world empires at the end of days, called
to judgment when God subjects all of humanity to the last judgment. But what about matters at the outset? Why did the gentiles
reject the Torah when it was given? To answer that question, story-
tellers turn to the first encounter, that is, the giving of the Torah
itself. In the timeless world constructed by the Judaic reading of

the Torah, what happens at the outset exemplifies how things always happen, and what happens at the end embodies what has always taken place. The basic thesis is identical – the gentiles cannot accept the Torah because to do so they would have to deny their very character.

Now the gentiles are not just Rome and Persia but others; and of special interest, the Torah is embodied in some of the Ten Commandments – those that are assigned to Adam and Noah, all humanity and not just Israel, as we saw earlier. These are, specifically, not to murder, not to commit adultery, not to steal; then the gentiles are rejected for not keeping the commandments assigned to the children of Noah. The upshot is that the reason that the gentiles rejected the Torah is that the Torah prohibits deeds that the gentiles do by their very nature.

SIFRÉ TO DEUTERONOMY CCCXLIII:IV.1FF.

A. Another teaching concerning the phrase, "He said, 'The Lord came from Sinai'":

B. When the Omnipresent appeared to give the Torah to Israel, it was not to Israel alone that he revealed himself but to every nation.

C. First of all he came to the children of Esau. He said to them, "Will you accept the Torah?"

D. They said to him, "What is written in it?"

E. He said to them, "'You shall not murder' (Exod. 20:13)."

F. They said to him, "The very being of 'those men' [namely, us] and of their father is to murder, for it is said, 'But the hands are the hands of Esau' (Gen. 27:22). 'By your sword you shall live' (Gen. 27:40)."

At this point we cover new ground: Other classes of gentiles that reject the Torah; now the Torah's own narrative takes over, replacing the known facts of world politics, such as the earlier account sets forth, and instead supplying evidence out of Scripture as to the character of the gentile group under discussion:

G. So he went to the children of Ammon and Moab and said to them, "Will you accept the Torah?"

H. They said to him, "What is written in it?"

I. He said to them, "'You shall not commit adultery' (Exod. 20:13)."

J. They said to him, "The very essence of fornication belongs to them [us], for it is said, 'Thus were both the daughters of Lot with child by their father' (Gen. 19:36)."

K. So he went to the children of Ishmael and said to them, "Will you accept the Torah?"

L. They said to him, "What is written in it?"

M. He said to them, "'You shall not steal' (Exod. 20:13)."

N. They said to him, "The very essence of their [our] father is thievery, as it is said, 'And he shall be a wild ass of a man' (Gen. 16:12)."

O. And so it went. He went to every nation, asking them, "Will you accept the Torah?"

P. For so it is said, "All the kings of the earth shall give you thanks, O Lord, for they have heard the words of your mouth" (Ps. 138:4).

Q. Might one suppose that they listened and accepted the Torah?

R. Scripture says, "And I will execute vengeance in anger and fury upon the nations, because they did not listen" (Mic. 5:14).

S. And it is not enough for them that they did not listen, but even the seven religious duties that the children of Noah indeed accepted upon themselves they could not uphold before breaking them.

T. When the Holy One, blessed be He, saw that that is how things were, he gave them to Israel.

At this point we turn back to the obligations that God has imposed upon the gentiles; these obligations have no bearing upon the acceptance of the Torah; they form part of the ground of being, the condition of existence of the gentiles. Yet even here, the gentiles do not accept God's authority even in matters of natural law.

FIVE GREAT OCCASIONS OF BASIC JUDAISM

Israel, thus, is what it is because of the Torah. Where does the Torah come to define matters? As we noted in the Preface, Judaism comes to expression through the calendar of holy days that governs the passage of the year. That calendar embodies the great events that Scripture records, those moments of eternity that frame Israel's existence then, now, always. In the repertoire of stories that Scripture sets forth, only a few figure in the annual reprise of Israel's life. Each of these has the power to transform the past into a moment in the here and now and turn contemporary Israelites into representatives of eternity. How the living embody the past is the lesson of basic Judaism.

I have chosen five such moments, which are spelled out in the law and lore that govern transactions of eternity in the cycle of the year, treated in the remainder of this chapter and the two that follow. Five great occasions basic to Judaism are, first, the Passover Seder, a home banquet that in springtime celebrates the Exodus of the Israelites from Egypt in ancient times, treated in Chapter 3. Then, second, in Chapter 4, we take up the story embodied in the Days of Awe, a synagogue rite that in the autumn marks the season of judgment, days of repentance, and atonement for sin, collective and individual. Then, third and fourth and fifth, all taken up in Chapter 5, come the Huppah or marriage canopy, the quite private rite of marriage of two Jewish individuals, and the rite of circumcision, than which there is no more personal rite – or more public one; and eating a meal.

Each rite recapitulates a segment of the Judaic narrative sustained and framed by Scripture. The first defines the relationship between the community of Israel and God, the second, between the individual Israelite and God, the third between one Israelite and another and the fourth between the male Israelite and God through the rite of circumcision. In all five instances, what we address is an acted-out narrative.

Since Judaism finds its definition both in books and in the life of the community of the faithful, we ask, "What about the practice of Judaism today – are these rites widely carried out?" The answer is yes. All are widely practiced. Surveys show that nearly all Jews – whether otherwise practitioners of Judaism or not – participate in a

Passover Seder of some sort. The vast majority of Judaists find their way to synagogue worship on the Days of Awe. In the State of Israel, the majority of the Jews who regard themselves as secular fast on the Day of Atonement, for example. When a Jew marries another Jew, it is highly likely to be under the auspices of Judaism.

For each occasion, we ask about the story that explains the event. We seek to derive from the rite and its companion myth (myth in the sense of truth in narrative form) the lessons about that encompassing religious system and structure, "Judaism," that are contained within the particular occasion at hand. We find that story in the liturgy of the occasion and shall uncover much repetition. For a well-articulated religion says the same thing about many things, and Judaism repeats its messages everywhere it turns.

THE SIGNALS OF NATURE, THE RESPONSE OF THE ISRAELITE

What signals do we seek? Events in the heavens and in human affairs convey the natural sounds of the narrative. For the first two of our selections of great occasions and their stories that define Judaism we turn to nature.

PASSOVER (CHAPTER 3)

The first full moon of spring, the one after March 21 of the solar calendar, the full moon of the lunar month of Nisan, signals the advent of the new barley crop. It also commemorates the liberation of the Israelite slaves from Egypt in the Exodus, "the season of our freedom" in the liturgy.

THE DAYS OF AWE, TABERNACLES (CHAPTER 4)

The Days of Awe commence on the first new moon prior to the first full moon after the autumnal equinox of September 21, the full moon of the lunar month of Tishré. That month is Judaism's holy season, beginning with the New Year, Rosh Hashanah, followed ten days later by the Day of Atonement, Yom Kippur, and five days after that, the full moon of the month marks the advent of the Festival of Tabernacles, Sukkot. That signals the climax of the great occasion that begins with new moon of Tishré. The first ten days of the lunar month of Tishré are called the Days of Awe.

At the full moon on the fifteenth of the month, the Festival of Tabernacles is celebrated with prayers for rain. Nature and the social order coincide. Bearing a message of God's judgment for the sins of the year past and his forgiveness for those that repent, the Days of Awe, the first ten days of Tishré, mark the season of judgment. That judgment comes in the form of bringing or withholding the winter rains, which secure sustenance for the year to come.

The upshot is simply stated. The two most important great occasions of the calendar of Judaism, Nisan / Passover and Tishré / the Days of Awe leading to Tabernacles, respond to the movement of the moon in the heavens in relationship to the solar seasons. But intensely particular narratives of Israel the community of Judaism mark those moments.

HUPPAH, CIRCUMCISION (BERIT MILAH), AND LUNCH (GRACE AFTER MEALS) (CHAPTER 5)

The third and fourth and fifth great occasions chosen to signal a basic story of Judaism are the Huppah, the marriage ceremony, and Berit Milah, the rite of circumcision into the Covenant of Abraham, and eating an ordinary meal, which invokes Heaven and Earth. The marriage ceremony translates what is personal into what is public, a foretaste of the rejoicing of all Israel at the restoration of Israel to the Land of Israel, corresponding to the return of Adam and Eve to Eden.

The signal of the third great occasion thus is private – a couple has chosen to create a new family. So, too, is the signal of the fourth, the advent of the newborn male child on the eighth day after birth. But the narrative of the Huppah invokes Eden, its loss and restoration, in the form of Israel, its loss of the Land of Israel and its restoration to the Land of Israel. The rite of circumcision is marked by a variety of scriptural narratives as well. The Grace after Meals is the most routine rite, and evokes the most intense moment of celebration. Now we have gotten ahead of ourselves. Let us start back with Passover, the story and the significance in the definition of the community of Judaism.

3

THE COMMUNITY OF JUDAISM AND PASSOVER

The celebration of Passover illustrates how the Israelite must see himself or herself as present in Israel's history through all eternity, so that even the living generation must regard itself as having been redeemed from Egypt. Through all time Israel depends on God's deliverance.

HOW PASSOVER DEFINES JUDAISM

At the festival of Passover, Jewish families gather around their tables for a holy meal. There they retell as an account of themselves and where they come from and who they are, the story of the Exodus from Egypt in times long past. They were slaves to Pharaoh in Egypt and God brought them out of bondage with an outstretched arm and a mighty hand. Therefore they celebrate – just as Scripture says – and tell the tale of liberation.

The single most widely practiced rite of Judaism and broadly celebrated by secular Jews as well requires family and friends to sit down together for a supper enlivened by stories. The meal is called the Seder, Order of Service, of Passover. The participants retell the story not only of the Exodus from Egypt but of their origins in the family of Abraham. Here is that fundamental moment of enchantment when ordinary people declare themselves to embody the Israel of which Scripture speaks.

The story is told in Exodus 1–15. The Israelites, children of Abraham, Isaac, and Jacob, in a time of famine, abandoned the Holy Land promised to Abraham's descendants. They went down to Egypt and stayed for a long time. Well treated at first, they were enslaved by the Pharaoh, King of Egypt. They cried out to God, and he called Moses to liberate them. After being smitten by ten plagues, Pharaoh allowed the Exodus to proceed. But he quickly changed his mind and pursued the fleeing slaves. The slaves reached the Red Sea, with the waves in front and the Egyptian chariots behind. They plunged into the waves, which opened before them, permitting them to pass on dry land, but which then closed upon and drowned the pursuing Egyptians. Saved at the sea, the Israelites sang a song to celebrate their salvation.

The Passover meal commemorates the salvation of Israel. How the narrative is set forth makes explicit the conception of Israel, the community of Judaism, that is acted out in the Seder.

THE LESSON OF PASSOVER

The lesson of Passover is drawn in the amplification of Deuteronomy 26:5–8 in light of the narrative of Exodus 1–11.

> A Syrian sought my father's death, but my father went down into Egypt with a handful of souls and sojourned there, and there he became a nation, great and powerful and mighty in number ... And we cried unto the Lord, the God of our fathers, and God heard our voice and beheld our torment and our travail and how we were oppressed.

Passover speaks of the family, of the fathers and mothers and how God intervened to save them from Egyptian bondage. The lesson then is that God answers prayer, attends to Israel's condition, and responds to that circumstance. That key verse is then glossed in a series of comments that amplify Scripture's record of the Exodus celebrated at Passover. I cite the base verse in small capitals, and the comment in regular type.

HE WENT DOWN INTO EGYPT [He did so by compulsion of the divine decree.]

Israel did not willingly give up the Land but followed God's instructions in migrating to Egypt. God gave Israel the Land of Israel, and Israel never relinquished its title to the Land, even to sojourn in Egypt].

AND SOJOURNED THERE [From which we learn that it was never his intention permanently to settle in Egypt ...]

The same point registers again: Israel left the Land only temporarily and remains outside of the Land only because of circumstance].

A HANDFUL OF SOULS ["With seventy souls your fathers went down into Egypt, and now the Lord your God has made you as the stars of heaven for number" (Deut. 10:22)].

AND WE CRIED UNTO THE LORD, THE GOD OF OUR FATHERS [We read in the Torah, "And in the course of those long years the king of Egypt died, and the children of Israel sighed in the midst of their slavery and wept and their complaint went up to God from the midst of their slavery" (Exod. 2:23)].

Israel became numerous in Egypt, but times changed and Israel was enslaved. God heard their cry:

AND GOD HEARD OUR VOICE [We are told, "And God heard their groaning and he remembered his covenant with Abraham, Isaac, and Jacob" (Exod. 2:24)] AND BEHELD OUR TORMENT [These words refer to the forcible separation of husbands and wives, for thus we understand the verse, "And God saw the children of Israel and God knew" (Exod. 2:25)] AND OUR TRAVAIL [This refers to the sons of the Israelites, for we read, "Every man child that is born to them you shall cast into the river and every daughter you shall save alive" (Exod. 1:22)] AND HOW WE WERE OPPRESSED [The crushing out of our life, according to the verse, "I have seen too the oppression which the Egyptians practice upon them" (Exod. 3:9)].

God responded by bringing Israel out of Egyptian bondage. This he did himself, not through an angel or an intermediary. His relationship with Israel is direct and intimate and immediate.

> "And God drew us forth from Egypt with a mighty hand and with an outstretched arm, in the midst of great awe, of portents and of wonders" (Deut. 26:8).

> AND GOD DREW US FORTH FROM EGYPT [He sent no intermediary, neither an angel nor a blazing seraph nor a messenger, it was God himself, blessed be he, in his glory. For we are told, "I will pass through the Land of Egypt in that night and I will smite all the first born of Egypt, man and beast, and I will execute judgment against all the gods of Egypt, I am the Lord" (Exod. 12:12)].

The amplification of the scriptural narrative reaches its climax with the statement, he sent no intermediary but came and saved Israel himself.

WHO AND WHAT IS ISRAEL?

Passover contains within its story and its rite Judaism's theory of who and what Israel is. The embodiment of Israel assembled for the festive Seder celebrates the Exodus, and to be "Israel" is to participate annually in the recapitulation of the miracle of freedom. With unleavened bread (for, as Scripture explains, the slaves fled in haste and had no time to allow dough to ferment) and sanctified wine, the gathered families celebrate the liberation of slaves from Pharaoh's bondage. What happens is not an act of memory but of reenactment, for this celebrates "the season of our freedom" not only theirs, long past:

> Forever after, in every generation, every Israelite must think of himself [or herself] as having gone forth from Egypt. For we read in the Torah, "In that day thou shalt teach thy child, saying, 'All this is because of what God did for me when I went forth from Egypt'" (Exod. 13:8). It was not only our ancestors that the Holy One, blessed be he, redeemed; us too the living, he redeemed together with them ...
>
> (Samuel 1942: 27)

The "we" of a family meal eaten in the shadow of the pyramids is transformed. The family is instructed to hold that it is in another time and another place. Nothing links present to past except an act of imagination: Pretend you are someone else, somewhere else. So each generation conceives of itself as comprised by slaves liberated from bondage – and finds in its contemporary situation the marks of oppression. That, unfortunately, has never been difficult to do.

The "Israel" of which Judaism speaks, then, represents in the here and now that very same Israel of which Scripture speaks. It continues the narrative begun in most ancient times. It forms the embodiment and contemporary continuation of that holy people, subject to God's love, of times past. And how is that realized? One theme stands out: We, here and now, are really living then and there. So for example in so many words the community declares:

> We were slaves of Pharaoh in Egypt and the Lord our God brought us forth from there with a mighty hand and an outstretched arm. And if the Holy One, blessed be he, had not brought our fathers forth from Egypt, then we and our descendants would still be slaves to Pharaoh in Egypt. And so, even if all of us were full of wisdom, understanding, sages and well informed in the Torah, we should still be obligated to repeat again the story of the Exodus from Egypt; and whoever treats as an important matter the story of the Exodus from Egypt is praiseworthy.
>
> (Samuel 1942: 9)

And again:

> This is the bread of affliction which our ancestors ate in the land of Egypt. Let all who are hungry come and eat with us, let all who are needy come and celebrate the Passover with us This year here, next year in the Land of Israel; this year slave, next year free people.
>
> (Samuel 1942: 8)

And yet a third statement:

> This is the promise which has stood by our forefathers *and stands by us*. For neither once, nor twice, nor three times was our destruction planned; in every generation they rise against us, and in every genera-

tion God delivers us from their hands into freedom, out of anguish
into joy, out of mourning into festivity, out of darkness into light, out
of bondage into redemption.

(Samuel 1942: 13)

In the aftermath of the Holocaust, that statement requires no
extension or amplification. Indeed, a rite of welcoming Elijah to the
Passover Seder takes on remarkable relevance. After the Passover
meal is served and grace is recited, the assembled family rises as a
door is opened for the advent of the prophet Elijah. A cup of wine is
set on the Seder table for Elijah. The family recites these verses of
Scripture:

"Pour out thine anger upon the nations that have not known you and
upon the kingdoms that do not call upon your name. For they have
devoured Jacob and laid waste his abode" (Ps. 79:6–7). "Pour out your
rage upon them, let your fury overtake them" (Ps. 69:25). "Pursue
them with the breath of your fury and destroy them from under the
heavens of the Lord" (Lam. 3:66) (trans. Samuel 1941: 41).

Elijah will join the family community in another celebration, the
circumcision on the eighth day after birth of Israelite males. Each
appearance bears its message. The appearance at the Passover Seder
invokes Elijah's task at the end of history, to inaugurate the judgment that is coming upon all creatures.

That is how the story of the Exodus turns out to impart meaning
to the anguish of later generations, especially the generation that
situates at the center of its memory the murder of nearly 6 million
Jews in German-occupied Europe in World War II: "In every
generation they rise against us." Somewhere, some time, that is
always so.

Accordingly, if I had in one sentence to explain the extraordinary
appeal of Passover in contemporary Judaism, it is in the this-
worldly, factual statement: We are hated, we are in trouble, but God
saves. Intensely relevant to the present age, Passover is popular now
because it speaks to a generation that knows what the gentiles can
do, having seen what they did to the Jews of Europe and how they
have singled out the State of Israel for "special handling." We shall
return to that matter in Chapter 11.

Passover, furthermore, speaks to not history alone but to personal biography. It joins together history with the experience of the individual. That is because the individual as a minority finds self-evident – relevant, true, urgent – a rite that reaches into the everyday and the here and now and turns that common world into a metaphor for the reality of Israel, enslaved but also redeemed. And that is what draws them to the Seder: It explains what, in the everyday, things mean beyond the 4 ells (square feet) of the private person's world. To be an Israelite, Judaism teaches, is to tell about oneself in private life the public narrative of Israel in nature and in history.

THE STORY OF PASSOVER PERPETUALLY PRESENT

What is the particular narrative of Passover? It starts from the very beginning:

> Long ago our ancestors were idol-worshippers but now the Holy One has drawn us to his service. So we read in the Torah: And Joshua said to all the people, "Thus says the Lord, God of Israel: From time immemorial your fathers lived beyond the river Euphrates, even to Terah, father of Abraham and of Nahor, and they worshipped idols. And I took your father Abraham from beyond the river and guided his footsteps throughout the land of Canaan. I multiplied his offspring and gave him Isaac. To Isaac I gave Jacob and Esau. And I set apart Mount Seir as the inheritance of Esau, while Jacob and his sons went down to Egypt" (Joshua 24:2–4).

> (Samuel 1942: 12)

Here is the second, and more important:

> Blessed is he who keeps his promise to Israel ... for the Holy One set a term to our bondage, fulfilling the word which he gave our father Abraham in the covenant made between the divided sacrifice: "Know beyond a doubt that your offspring will be strangers in a land that is not theirs, four hundred years they shall serve and suffer. But in the end I shall pronounce judgment on the oppressor people and your offspring shall go forth with great wealth" (Gen. 15:13–14).

> (Samuel 1942: 12)

When Jewish people say of themselves, "We were the slaves of Pharaoh in Egypt," their liberation, not merely that of long-dead forebears, they now celebrate. The power of the Passover banquet rite to transform ordinary existence into an account of something beyond lies here. That deliverance is not at a single moment in historical time. It is a model, a pattern, of what happens all the time. Transformed into a permanent feature of reality, it is made myth, truth in narrative form – that story of deep truth that comes true in every generation and is always celebrated. Here again, events of natural, ordinary life are transformed through myth into paradigmatic, eternal, and ever-recurrent sacred moments. The everyday is treated as a paradigm and a metaphor. Israelites think of themselves as having gone forth from Egypt, and Scripture so instructs them. God did not redeem the dead generation of the Exodus alone, but the living too – especially the living. Thus the family states:

> Again and again, in double and redoubled measure, are we beholden to God the All-Present: That He freed us from the Egyptians and wrought His judgment on them; that He sentenced all their idols and slaughtered all their first-born; that He gave their treasure to us and split the Red Sea for us; that He led us through it dry-shod and drowned the tyrants in it; that He helped us through the desert and fed us with the manna; that He gave the Sabbath to us and brought us to Mount Sinai; that He gave the Torah to us and brought us to our homeland – there to build the Temple for us, for atonement of our sins.
>
> (Samuel 1942: 26)

Note the catalogue of stories that are rehearsed: Freedom from slavery, punishment of the Egyptians for their idolatry, splitting of the Red Sea, maintaining Israel in the wilderness, then comes the Sabbath, Sinai and the giving of the Torah, the restoration to the Land of Israel and the building of the temple – a continuous story of Israel's salvation. Whatever "really" happened in secular history plays no role. Here we deal with things that God did, a narrative of salvation that does not bear upon this world but upon divine intervention, which has left its mark in time, upon history. The four cups of wine that are drunk by each celebrant of the Passover stand for four moments in history.

The redemptive promise that stood by the forefathers and "stands by us" is not a mundane historical event, but a mythic interpretation of natural events that are beyond historical recovery. The myth that a Jew must think of himself or herself as having gone forth from Egypt and as being redeemed by God renders ordinary experience into a moment of celebration. If "us, too, the living, He redeemed," then the observer no longer witnesses only historical folk in historical time, but an eternal return to sacred time.

THE ISRAELITE BEFORE GOD AND THE DAYS OF AWE

Judaism speaks not only of corporate Israel, the community, but of the individual Israelite. That requires a different narrative, one that speaks of personal biographies, individual repentance, atonement, and forgiveness. That is what the Days of Awe, the New Year, and the Day of Atonement, followed by the Festival of Tabernacles, "the season of our rejoicing," provide. The Days of Awe fall on the first day of the lunar month of Tishré, for the New Year / Rosh Hashanah, the tenth day of that same month, for the Day of Atonement / Yom Kippur, and the fifteenth day of that same lunar month, the full moon, for Tabernacles / Sukkot. The New Year is the birthday of the world. Then everybody is judged. The Day of Atonement is a day of forgiveness for sin. The key narrative of the Days of Awe is built on Genesis 22, the binding of Isaac, and God's remembrance, on behalf of Abraham's descendants, of that act of supreme sacrifice. Tabernacles commemorates the sojourn in huts in the wilderness for forty years.

A DIFFERENT KIND OF NARRATIVE

The story of who and what is Israel records public events, the Passover narrative speaks of all Israel, the corporate community.

The Days of Awe, the New Year, and the Day of Atonement, with their climax at the Festival of Tabernacles, by contrast, bear a deeply personal message, one of sin and punishment, atonement and forgiveness. Everyone is subject one by one to God's judgment, and everyone comes before God to be inscribed in the Book of Life for the coming year. The focus is on individuals and their standing before God.

Now a different narrative model takes over. It is the story of God and one man, who is Abraham, the first Israelite. Once more, we turn to Scripture for the story, and to the rabbinic sages of classical Judaism for the adaptation of the story to the theological program of Judaism.

It is, specifically, Scripture's story at Genesis 22, which tells how God tested Abraham and so commanded Abraham to offer up Isaac, his son, as an offering. Abraham was prepared to do so, and Isaac affirmed his calling as a sacrifice. God at the last moment provided a ram for an offering in place of Isaac. Declaimed in the synagogue on the second day of the New Year or Rosh Hashanah, the Judaic reading of the story links it to the theme of Israelites subject to divine justice. How this ultimate act of submission to God's will relates to Rosh Hashanah and Yom Kippur, and so forms the narrative of the Israelite before God, is spelled out in the setting of God's judgment of all humanity.

THE NARRATIVE OF THE DAYS OF AWE: THE NEW YEAR, THE DAY OF REMEMBRANCE

On Rosh Hashanah, the Shofar or ram's horn is sounded, and why this is the case is explained in a narrative that contains the key to the relationship between the Israelite and God when he judges Israel. The story of Genesis 22 has God call Abraham to take his son Isaac to the place he will show him, Moriah, which is the future temple mount, and to offer him as a burnt offering. Abraham complies. The climax of the story is told as follows:

> When they came to the place of which God had told him, Abraham built an altar there and laid the wood in order and bound Isaac his son and laid him on the altar, upon the wood. Then Abraham put forth his hand and took the knife to slay his son. But the angel of the Lord

called to him from heaven and said, "Abraham, Abraham!" And he said, "Here am I." He said, "Do not lay your hand on the lad or do anything to him, for now I know that you fear God, seeing you have not withheld your son, your only son, from me."

(Gen. 22:9–12)

Now comes the ancient rabbinic commentary on the narrative which explicitly carries us to the Days of Awe. It is from Genesis Rabbah, a commentary on the book of Genesis, which came to closure at *c.* 450 C.E. Here, the Shofar is sounded to arouse God's sympathy, his memory of not only the sins of the Israelites but also the merit of their ancestor, Abraham. That represents a powerful initiative in reshaping the story.

The passage involves citing a verse of Genesis and glossing that verse, specifically by quoting other verses of Scripture, here deriving from Zechariah, the biblical prophet, to amplify the statement of Genesis. The rabbis who are cited flourished in the third and fourth centuries C.E. and read Scripture in the light of the destruction of the Second Temple in 70 and in the rabbinic conception that the all-merciful God judges and forgives Israel when Israel repents.

Genesis Rabbah LVI:IX

A. "And Abraham lifted up his eyes and looked, and behold, behind him was a ram, [caught in a thicket by his horns. And Abraham went and took the ram and offered it up as a burnt offering instead of his son]" (Gen. 22:13).

B. What is the meaning of the word for "behind"?

C. Said R. Yudan, "'Behind' in the sense of 'after,' that is, after all that happens, Israel nonetheless will be embroiled in transgressions and perplexed by sorrows. But in the end, they will be redeemed by the horns of a ram: 'And the Lord will blow the horn' (Zech. 9:14)."

The Shofar is sounded to signal the redemption of Israel. "Behind him" means, after all that has happened, despite it all Israel will be redeemed.

> D.   Said R. Judah bar Simon, "'After' all generations Israel nonetheless will be embroiled in transgressions and perplexed by sorrows. But in the end, they will be redeemed by the horns of a ram: 'And the Lord God will blow the horn' (Zech. 9:14)."

Now "after" means even at the last generations, Israel will be redeemed in the end of days.

> E.   Said R. Hinena bar Isaac, "All through the days of the year Israelites are embroiled in transgressions and perplexed by sorrows. But on the New Year they take the ram's horn and sound it, so in the end, they will be redeemed by the horns of a ram: 'And the Lord God will blow the horn' (Zech. 9:14)."

The same general trend continues, now with reference to after all that happens through the days of the year, rather than after history or after all generations.

> F.   R. Abba bar R. Pappi, R. Joshua of Siknin in the name of R. Levi: "Since our father, Abraham, saw the ram get himself out of one thicket only to be trapped in another, the Holy One, blessed be he, said to him, 'So your descendants will be entangled in one kingdom after another, struggling from Babylonia to Media, from Media to Greece, from Greece to Edom. But in the end, they will be redeemed by the horns of a ram: And the Lord God will blow the horn ... the Lord of Hosts will defend them' (Zech. 9:14–15)."

The interpretation of the passage shifts in character. Now the image of the ram entangled in the bush conveys the picture of Israel entangled in the affair of the world empires, Babylonia, Media, Greece, Edom meaning Rome, the sequence of four world empires that the rabbinic sages believed would end their rule with the advent of God's rule of all humanity. With the sounding of the ram's horn, God's ultimate rule commences. The story of Abraham and Isaac on Moriah, which is the temple mount of Jerusalem, accordingly encompasses their descendants, the Israelites, who will be crashing from thicket to thicket, from subjugation to one kingdom to that of another. But finally the great Shofar will be sounded for their redemption.

The power of the opening reading is to link the life of the private person, affected by transgression, and the history of the nation, troubled by its wandering among the kingdoms. From the perspective of the Land of Israel, the issue is not exile but the rule of foreigners. In both cases, the power of the ram's horn to redeem the individual and the nation finds its origin in the binding of Isaac. The interpretation of the rabbinic commentators links the lives of the patriarchs to the life of the nation. That reading brings the narrative back to the setting of individual being, so from patriarch to nation to person.

Now we come to the great narrative of divine judgment: The Day of Remembrance, when God remembers what everyone has done and judges accordingly. What has the ram's horn to do with the Day of Remembrance? Is it to be God's recalling sin or God's recalling the merit of Abraham's faith in judging Abraham's offspring? Here is the answer.

Genesis Rabbah LVI:X

> A. "So Abraham called the name of that place 'The Lord will provide,' [as it is said to this day, 'On the mount of the Lord it shall be provided']" (Gen. 22:14).
>
> B. R. Bibi the Elder in the name of R. Yohanan: "He said before him, 'Lord of all ages, from the time that you said to me, "Take your son, your only son" (Gen. 22:2), I could have replied to you, "Yesterday you said to me, 'For in Isaac shall seed be called to you' (Gen. 21:12), and now you say, 'Take your son, your only son' (Gen. 22:2). God forbid, did I not do it? But I suppressed my love so as to carry out your will. May it always please you, Lord our God, that, when the children of Isaac will come into trouble,

> you remember in their behalf that act of binding
> and be filled with mercy for them."

There is no mystery to the rabbinic reading of the narrative. In so many words the point is spelled out: "When the children of Isaac will come into trouble, you remember." The narrative of the Days of Awe encompasses the loyalty and faith of Abraham and of Isaac, the one to sacrifice, the other to be sacrificed, in the test of faith. Now God responds even while judging the descendants.

So Judaism tells the story of not only corporate Israel, the community of Judaism, but also of individual Israelites and of how, in the light of the conduct of Abraham and Isaac, each individual is judged by God. The liturgy translates the story into a series of descriptive statements. On the first day of the lunar year, the new moon of Tishré, all humanity passes before God and is judged for the year to come. It is the day of remembrance, on which each person's deeds are weighed in the balance, for judgment. The prayers for the New Year eloquently state matters:

> On this day sentence is passed upon countries, which to the sword and which to peace, which to famine and which to plenty, and each creature is judged today for life or death. Who is not judged on this day? For the remembrance of every creature comes before You, each one's deeds and destiny, words and way ...

That is how the liturgy states the theology of the Days of Awe. But the story contains other chapters, all of which form a single statement.

ROSH HASHANAH, THE NEW YEAR: THE BIRTHDAY OF THE WORLD

The great themes of the synagogue liturgy for the New Year tell the tale of God as judge in three aspects: God's remembrance (of Abraham and Isaac, of acts of merit and of sins), God's dominion or kingship, thus God as judge, and God's sounding the Shofar to announce the redemption of Israel. Then, judging the world for the coming year, God asserts his sovereignty, as in the New Year Prayer:

> Our God and God of our Fathers, Rule over the whole world in Your honor ... and appear in Your glorious might to all those who dwell in the civilization of Your world, so that everything made will know that You made it, and every creature discern that You have created him, so that all in whose nostrils is breath may say, "The Lord, the God of Israel is king, and His kingdom extends over all."

God is creator. He reveals the Torah. He will redeem humanity in the end of days. Thus, God created the world and rules, God is made manifest in the Torah, and God will in the end of days redeem humanity from the condition of sin and death brought about by Adam's failure. At the end, God will accord eternal life to his dominion. God's sovereignty is established by creation of the world. Judgment depends upon law: "From the beginning You made this, Your purpose known." And, therefore, since people have been told what God requires of them, they are judged:

> On this day sentence is passed upon countries, which to the sword and which to peace, which to famine and which to plenty, and each creature is judged today for life or death. Who is not judged on this day? For the remembrance of every creature comes before You, each man's deeds and destiny, words and way.

The theme of revelation is further combined with redemption; the ram's horn, or Shofar, which is sounded in the synagogue during daily worship for a month before the Rosh Hashanah festival, serves to unite the two:

> You did reveal yourself in a cloud of glory ... Out of heaven you made them [Israel] hear Your voice ... Amid thunder and lightning You revealed yourself to them, and while the Shofar sounded You shined forth upon them ... Our God and God of our fathers, sound the great Shofar for our freedom. Lift up the ensign to gather our exiles ... Lead us happily to Zion Your city, Jerusalem the place of Your sanctuary.

The complex themes of the New Year thus involve God as king, God as redeemer, God as judge with a very good memory for all that happens. The liturgy with its narrative of divine judgment and forgiveness thus weaves together in the tapestry of a highly charged moment in a world subject to the personal scrutiny of a most active God.

The time of new beginnings also marks endings: On the New Year the decree is issued: Who will live and who will die? At the New Year – so the words state – humanity is inscribed for life or death in the heavenly books for the coming year, and on the Day of Atonement the books are sealed. The synagogues on that day are filled. The New Year is a day of remembrance on which the deeds of all creatures are reviewed. The principal themes of the words invoke creation, and God's rule over creation, revelation, and God's rule in the Torah for the created world, and redemption, God's ultimate plan for the world.

Liturgical words concerning divine sovereignty, divine memory, and divine disclosure correspond to creation, revelation, and redemption. Sovereignty is established by creation of the world. Judgment depends upon law: "From the beginning You made this, Your purpose known ... " And therefore, since people have been told what God requires of them, they are judged.

The dominant narrative has shown how the theme of revelation is further combined with redemption; the ram's horn, or Shofar, which is sounded in the synagogue during daily worship for a month before the Rosh Hashanah festival, serves to unite the two:

> You did reveal yourself in a cloud of glory ... Out of heaven you made them [Israel] hear Your voice ... Amid thunder and lightning You revealed yourself to them, and while the Shofar sounded You shined forth upon them ... Our God and God of our fathers, sound the great Shofar for our freedom. Lift up the ensign to gather our exiles ... Lead us happily to Zion Your city, Jerusalem the place of Your sanctuary.

What of the Day of Atonement? Here too we hear the same answers, see the unfolding of a single process of transformation of secular into sacred time.

YOM KIPPUR, THE DAY OF ATONEMENT

A day of fasting and prayer, second in popular observance only to the Passover Seder, Yom Kippur is the most widely observed rite of Judaism among Judaists and widely observed by ethnic Jews as well.

So on it the vast majority of Jews in the world find their way to
corporate Israel assembled in synagogue worship – and there they
speak of themselves, individuals within the community, Israelites of
Israel the holy people.

The most solemn, and moving of the Days of Awe, the Day of
Atonement, the Sabbath of Sabbaths, is marked by fasting and
nearly continuous prayer.

> On the Day of Atonement it is forbidden to (1) eat, (2) drink, (3) bathe,
> (4) put on any sort of oil, (5) put on a sandal, (6) or engage in sexual
> relations (M. Yoma 8:1A).

The Day of Atonement *by its very advent* at sunset at the eve of
the tenth of the lunar month of Tishré atones for sin, along with
repentance – regret for sin, resolution not to repeat it – prayer and
fasting. This is spelled out in Box 4.1.

BOX 4.1 HOW THE DAY OF ATONEMENT ATONES

Tosefta Kippurim 4:5

M. Death and the Day of Atonement effect atonement
   along with repentance.

N. Repentance effects atonement for minor transgressions of positive and negative commandments [M.
   Yoma 8:8B-C], except for a violation of the commandment not to take [the name of the Lord in vain].

O. And what are major transgressions? [Those punish-
   able by] extirpation and death at the hands of an
   earthly court, and 'not taking [the name of the Lord in
   vain]' counts with them.

P. R Judah says, "For everything from 'not taking [the
   name of the Lord in vain]' and beneath, repentance
   effects atonement.

Q. "For everything from 'not taking [the name of the
   Lord in vain]' and above, inclusive of 'not taking
   [the name of the Lord in vain],' repentance suspends
   the punishment, and the Day of Atonement effects
   atonement."

What accounts for the power of the Day of Atonement to atone for sin? It is not the rites of the day, nor the act of refraining from food, drink, and sex. The advent of the day itself bears that remarkable power. That is broadly recognized among Jews. Secular Jews who otherwise throughout the year do not practice the rites of Judaism observe the prohibitions of the day and find their way to the synagogue.

The theme of the fate of the individual Israelite, not only the entire community of Israel, predominates. Scripture declares the Day of Atonement the day that brings forgiveness for sin:

> It shall be a statute for you for ever that in the seventh month, on the tenth day of the month, you shall afflict yourself and shall do no work, either the native or the stranger who sojourns among you; for on this day shall atonement be made for you, to cleanse you, from all your sins you shall be clean before the Lord.
>
> (Lev. 16:32–4)

NEW BEGINNINGS ON THE DAY OF ATONEMENT

The holy day begins with a public remission of the past year's vows, so that the congregants may appear before God unencumbered by vows that, thoughtlessly, they have taken to God in the year now coming to a close.

> All vows and oaths we take, all promises and obligations we make between this Day of Atonement and the next we hereby publicly retract in the event that we should forget them and hereby declare our intention to be absolved of them.

Sung at sunset on the eve of the Day of Atonement, the formula called Kol Nidré, for the opening words, "All vows," scarcely understood for the trivial pledge that it contains, moves masses of Jews to come to synagogue who otherwise scarcely find their way there. The Israelite individual makes confession:

> Our God and God of our fathers, may our prayer come before You. Do not hide yourself from our supplication, for we are not so arrogant or

stiff-necked as to say before You ... We are righteous and have not sinned. But we have sinned. We are guilt laden, we have been faithless, we have robbed ... We have committed iniquity, caused unrighteousness, have been presumptuous ... We have counseled evil, scoffed, revolted, blasphemed.

The Hebrew confession is built upon an alphabetical acrostic, as if by making certain every letter is represented, God, who knows human secrets, will combine them into appropriate words. The very alphabet bears witness against us before God. Then:

What shall we say before You who dwell on high? What shall we tell You who live in heaven? Do You not know all things, both the hidden and the revealed? You know the secrets of eternity, the most hidden mysteries of life. You search the innermost recesses, testing people's feelings and heart. Nothing is concealed from You or hidden from Your eyes. May it therefore be Your will to forgive us our sins, to pardon us for our iniquities, to grant remission for our transgressions.

A further list of sins follows, built on alphabetical lines. Prayers to be spoken by the congregation are all in the plural: "For the sin which we have sinned against You with the utterance of the lips ... For the sin which we have sinned before You openly and secretly." The community takes upon itself responsibility for what is done in it. All Israel is part of one community, one body, and all are responsible for the acts of each. The sins confessed are mostly against society, against one's fellow human beings; few pertain to ritual laws. At the end comes a final word:

O my God, before I was formed, I was nothing. Now that I have been formed, it is as though I had not been formed, for I am dust in my life, more so after death. Behold I am before You like a vessel filled with shame and confusion. May it be Your will ... that I may no more sin, and forgive the sins I have already committed in Your abundant compassion.

While much of the liturgy speaks of "we," the individual focus dominates, beginning to end. The Days of Awe speak to the heart of the individual, telling a story of judgment and atonement. So the individual Jew stands before God: Possessing no merits, yet hopeful of God's love and compassion.

But the season does not close yet. The fate of the community is being decided even now. Nature forms the arena of judgment. The rainy season in the Land of Israel, on which all life depends for crops for the coming year in biblical times, begins shortly. Judgment is no abstraction. Israel is judged for the year now commencing, and the abundance of rains will carry out that judgment. Prayers for rain take a prominent role in the liturgy of the festival now coming up.

SUKKOT / THE FESTIVAL OF TABERNACLES

Five days later, after the Day of Atonement, on the fifteenth of the lunar month of Tishré, at the first full moon after the autumnal equinox, falls Tabernacles or Sukkot, seven days in duration, like Passover. (In the Diaspora, Passover and Tabernacles last for eight days, in the State of Israel, as Scripture requires, seven.) The narrative shifts to represent Israel now as a pilgrim people, wandering in the wilderness, expiating the sin of a generation that rebelled against God. It is that aspect of the Festival of Tabernacles that concerns us here: The meaning of the *sukkah*, or hut, itself.

Here is yet another story, not continuous with the narrative of Rosh Hashanah and Yom Kippur but equally definitive. The Festival of Tabernacles places Israel beyond the sea and Sinai, wandering about in the wilderness, where by reason of rebellion against God, Israel sojourned for forty years. Israel then is reminded that it is a people who have sinned, but that God can and does forgive.

The sojourn in the wilderness embodies the story. There they remained until the entire generation of the wilderness had died out, and Israel was ready to enter the Land. Passover places Israel's freedom into the context of the affirmation of life beyond sin, Sukkot returns Israel to the fragility of abiding in the wilderness, as Moses explicitly states. Leviticus 23:33–43 defines the festival:

> And the Lord said to Moses, "Say to the people of Israel, On the fifteenth day of this seventh month and for seven days is the feast of Tabernacles to the Lord ... You shall dwell in Tabernacles for seven days; all that are native in Israel shall dwell in Tabernacles, that your

generations may know that I made the people of Israel dwell in Tabernacles when I brought them out of the land of Egypt; I am the Lord your God."

So the story, told in separate chapters, presents a discontinuous narrative, each part making its own point, the whole held together by the movement of the sun and the moon in the heavens.

Now Israel is wandering in the wilderness, after the exalted messages of the New Year and the Day of Atonement, the narrative jars; it is not what we should have expected. To know why that is so, we must recall the Scriptural narrative, with its explanation for why Israel had to wander for forty years in the wilderness. It was a journey that can have been completed in a few weeks, even by a massive caravan. But what happened, so Deuteronomy (1:19–37) tells us, is that the Israelites approached the Land and sent out rangers to report on its condition. But the people sulked and did not believe they could prevail (Deut. 1:26, 34–5):

Yet you would not go up but rebelled against the command of the Lord your God ... And the Lord heard your words and was angered and he swore, "Not one of these men of this evil generation shall see the good land that I swore to give to your fathers."

On that account, Israel wandered for forty years in the wilderness, and the Festival of Tabernacles reminds Israel of how by reason of its rebellion, it lived in temporary hovels for an entire generation.

The principal observance of the festival is the construction of a Sukkah, the Hebrew word for a frail hut, for temporary use as a sometime shelter. In it Israel lives once more in the condition of that sinful generation, eating meals and (where the climate permits) sleeping out of doors. What defines the hut is the roofing, which must cast more shade than light, but not be fully covered over. Roofing of branches, leaves, fruit, and flowers allows light to show through, and at night, the stars. At this time of the renewal of the fructifying rains, it is good to be reminded of man's travail and dependence upon heavenly succor. The hut or Sukkah is an abode that cannot serve in the rainy season that is coming, announced by the new moon that occasions the festival. Israel is to take shelter, in reverting to the wilderness, in any random ramshackle hut, covered with what nature has provided but in form and in purpose what man otherwise does not value.

The temporary abode of the Israelite, the Sukkah, in its transience matches Israel's condition in the wilderness, wandering between Egypt and the Land, death and eternal life. Just as Passover marks the differentiation of Israel, expiating sin through the Passover offering and so attaining life, from Egypt, expiating sin through the death of the first-born, so Tabernacles / Sukkot addresses the condition of Israel. The story concerns the generation of the wilderness, that is the generation that must die out before Israel can enter the Land. So, entering the Sukkah reminds Israel not only of the fragility of its condition but also – in the aftermath of the penitential season – of its actuality.

What the Festival of Tabernacles, at the end of the penitential season, registers is the fragility and culpability of liberated, covenanted Israel. The present tense takes over, for the community of Israel is required to make its residence a temporary hut. Israelites see themselves as liberated from Egypt and as present at Sinai. Tabernacles continues the pattern of living in the presence of the past. Now to the ultimate question: How does the individual Israelite embody the narrative of all Israel?

5

THE INDIVIDUAL ISRAELITE AND ISRAEL IN HISTORY

The Huppah; the Covenant of Abraham; eating lunch

The story of Israel in history is told in the private and personal chapters of the lives of individuals. The wedding rite ("huppah" marriage canopy) refers the bride and groom to Adam and Eve, and to the destruction of the temple of Jerusalem, and the coming restoration of Israel to the Land of Israel at the end of days. Jeremiah's message of hope at the moment of despair before the fall of the first temple is recited.

The Covenant of Abraham, the rite of circumcision, calls to mind the prophet Elijah, who comes to witness the loyalty of the Israelites to the covenant as shown by the rite of circumcision.

Every meal ends with a grace that speaks of Creation, Exodus, the Land, Restoration and Redemption – the entire repertoire of stories is rehearsed on the humble and private occasion of eating lunch.

The individual Israelite figures in the narratives of the community, and specific moments in private life are turned by the prayers that are recited into public events. Marriage and circumcision represent highly private occasions that are transformed by the Israelite stories into moments in the story of the community of Israel. Even more to the point, Grace, recited after meals, reviews the great themes of Creation, Exodus, the Land and Restoration. So eating a meal invokes the narrative of corporate Israel. At home and in the family, the Israelite is always ready to tell the stories that convey the basics of Judaism, the definition of who and what is Israel, the meaning of the principal parts of the way of life, the narratives that capture principal parts and elements of the worldview.

HOW THE MARRIAGE RITE (HUPPAH) DEFINES THE BRIDE AND GROOM WITHIN THE NARRATIVES OF JUDAISM

The narrative of the marriage liturgy transforms into the public life of Israel the space, time, action of the "I" of the groom and the "I" of the bride. The "we," the family coming into being, is made to embody all Israel. The space is contained by the *huppah*, translated as marriage canopy, which (when done correctly) is constructed under the open sky – a contained space of heaven representing heavenly Eden. The time is now "in the beginning." The action then invokes creation, the making of a new Eden. The community of the two "I"s becoming one "we" is the couple changed into the paradigm of humanity, beginning with Adam and Eve. So the union of woman and man becomes the beginning of a new creation, so that the woman becomes Eve, the man, Adam.

The rite makes explicit reference to Adam and Eve in recognizing the groom and bride and blessing them. It also invokes the complement to Adam and Eve, which is Israel: Eden and temple match. But the occasion dictates hope. The destruction of the temple calls to mind at the Huppah only the hope, presaged here and now, of restoration at the end of days.

Thus, two distinct Israelite narratives joined together for this occasion. The first invokes the story of the new representation of Eden with Adam and Eve given a second chance. The second evokes Israel's joy of redemption, the restoration that is adumbrated in the joy of groom and bride.

The rite unfolds in stages, beginning before the couple reaches the marriage canopy. If we walk through the rite, stopping at its stages, we come first to the touching moment at which the groom places the veil over the bride's face, prior to the entry into the marriage canopy, and makes the following statement to her:

> May you, our sister, be fruitful and prosper. May God make you as Sarah, Rebecca, Rachel, and Leah. May the Lord bless you and keep you. May the Lord show you favor and be gracious to you. May the Lord show you kindness and grant you peace.

> (Harlow 1965: 32–3)

The blessing of the groom for the bride invokes the matriarchs of Israel. We need not find this detail surprising. Each rite we have examined treats the Israelite as the embodiment in the here and now of a figure drawn from the narrative of the Torah, a child of Abraham and Isaac, here, the representative of the matriarchs of the scriptural narrative.

At the climax comes the recitation of Seven Blessings (*sheva berakhot*). Here are those seven transforming statements of sanctification said over a cup of wine:

> Praised are You, O Lord our God, King of the universe, Creator of the fruit of the vine.

Three blessings follow, which invoke the theme of Adam and Eve and which explain the transaction at hand by appeal to the story of the creation of Eve:

> Praised are You, O Lord our God, King of the universe, who created all things for Your glory.
> Praised are You, O Lord our God, King of the universe, Creator of Adam.
> Praised are You, O Lord our God, King of the universe, who created man and woman in his image, fashioning woman from man as his mate, that together they might perpetuate life. Praised are You, O Lord, Creator of man.

The theme of paradise is introduced by the simple choice of the word "Adam." The sequence of themes is, first, creation of all things, then, creation of man, then, creation of man and woman in God's image. These words invoke the moments out of eternity for which the occasion at hand serves as metaphor. Israel's story begins with creation – first, the creation of the vine, symbol of the natural world. Creation is for God's glory. In Hebrew, the blessings end, "who formed the Adam." The story of man's creation is rehearsed: Man and woman are in God's image, together complete and whole, creators of life, "like God." Woman was fashioned from man together with him to perpetuate life. And again, "blessed is the creator of Adam." We have moved, therefore, from the natural world to the archetypal realm of paradise. Before us we see not merely a man and a woman, but Adam and Eve.

Next comes a jarring intrusion: The condition of Zion in the context of creation! The rejoicing of Adam and Eve finds its mirror in the joy that is coming to the mother, Zion:

> May Zion rejoice as her children are restored to her in joy. Praised are You, O Lord, who causes Zion to rejoice at her children's return.

This Adam and this Eve also are Israel, children of Zion the mother. Zion lies in ruins, her children scattered. Adam and Eve cannot celebrate together without thought to the condition of the mother, Jerusalem. The children will one day come home. The joy of the moment gives a foretaste of the joy of restoration, redemption, return. Now the two roles become one in that same joy, first Adam and Eve, groom and bride, Eden then, the marriage canopy now:

> Grant perfect joy to these loving companions, as You did to the first man and woman in the Garden of Eden. Praised are You, O Lord, who grants the joy of bride and groom.

That same joy comes in the metaphors of Zion the bride and Israel the groom. But this is made very specific, alluding to the vision of Jeremiah. On the eve of the destruction of the first temple in 586 B.C.E., he prophesied when all seemed lost, that Jerusalem, about to fall and lose its people, will one day ring with the shouts of not the slaughtered and the enslaved but the returned and redeemed. That is why the concluding blessing returns to the theme of Jerusalem. This time it evokes the tragic hour of Jerusalem's first destruction. When everyone had given up hope, supposing with the end of Jerusalem had come the end of time, only Jeremiah (33:10–11) counseled renewed hope. With the enemy at the gate, he sang of coming gladness:

> Thus says the Lord: In this place of which you say, "It is a waste, without man or beast," in the cities of Judah and the streets of Jerusalem that are desolate, without man or inhabitant or beast, there shall be heard again the voice of mirth and the voice of gladness, the voice of the bridegroom and the voice of the bride, the voice of those who sing as they bring thank-offerings to the house of the Lord ... For I shall restore the fortunes of the land as at first, says the Lord.

Three moments mix in the final blessing, past, present, and future: Eden then, marriage party now, and Zion in the coming age:

> Praised are You, O Lord our God, King of the universe, who created joy and gladness, bride and groom, mirth, song, delight and rejoicing, love and harmony, peace and companionship. O Lord our God, may there ever be heard in the cities of Judah and in the streets of Jerusalem voices of joy and gladness, voices of bride and groom, the jubilant voices of those joined in marriage under the bridal canopy, the voices of young people feasting and singing.
> Praised are You, O Lord, who causes the groom to rejoice with his bride.

The closing blessing defines the jubilant climax of this acted-out narrative: Just as here and now there stand before us Adam and Eve, so here and now in this wedding, the olden sorrow having been rehearsed, we listen to the voice of gladness that is coming. Zion the bride, Israel the groom, united now as they will be reunited by the compassionate God – these stand under the marriage canopy.

What we learn about Judaism from the narrative of the Huppah is how religion works. Invoking creation, Adam and Eve, the Garden of Eden, Jerusalem in ruins and Jerusalem restored, takes ordinary events and turns them into moments of eternity in time. Here is how religion serves as a means of ultimate transformation, rendering the commonplace into the paradigmatic, changing the here and now into a moment of eternity and of eternal return. The marriage liturgy serves to exemplify the communion of the ages, the shared being of all who have lived as Israel.

HOW THE RITE OF THE COVENANT OF ABRAHAM (CIRCUMCISION) DEFINES THE NEWBORN SON WITHIN THE NARRATIVES OF JUDAISM

A story transforms the birth of the male child from a private happening in the natural family to a public and momentous event in the life of the supernatural family of Israel on earth and of God in heaven. A minor surgical procedure, in Hebrew, Berit Milah, the covenant of circumcision, removal of the foreskin of the penis of the male child on the eighth day after birth, becomes the mark of the renewal of the agreement between God and Israel, the covenant carved into the flesh of the penis of every Jewish male.

The beginning of a new life renews the rule that governs Israel's relationship to God. So the private joy is transformed into renewal of the community of Israel and God. Circumcision must take place on the eighth day after birth, as Abraham did with Isaac: "Abraham circumcised his son Isaac when he was eight days old, as God had commanded him" (Gen. 21:4). It is in the presence of a quorum of ten.

There are four aspects in which the operation is turned into a rite. When the rite begins, the assembly and the *mohel* together recite the following:

> The Lord spoke to Moses saying, "Phineas, son of Eleazar, son of Aaron, the priest, has turned my wrath from the Israelites by displaying among them his passion for me, so that I did not wipe out the Israelite people in my passion. Say therefore I grant him my covenant of peace."

> (Num. 25:11)

Commenting on this passage, Lifsa Schachter states,

> Phineas is identified with zealously opposing the ... sins of sexual licentiousness and idolatry. He is best known for an event which occurred when the Israelites, whoring with Moabite women in the desert, were drawn to the worship of Baal-Peor ... Phineas leaped into the fray and through an act of double murder ... quieted God's terrible wrath.

> (Schachter 1986: 41)

Second, in looking around the room where the rite takes place, we notice that a chair is set called "the chair of Elijah." The newborn son is set on that chair, and the congregation says, "This is the chair of Elijah, of blessed memory." Why introduce the narrative of Elijah the prophet? Elijah had complained to God that Israel neglected the covenant (1 Kgs. 19:10–14). So he comes to bear witness that Israel observes the covenant of circumcision. Then, we see, before the surgical operation, a blessing is said. Third, we note, after the operation, a blessing is said over a cup of wine. Let us take up each of these three matters and explore their meaning. To understand the invocation of Elijah, we first recall the pertinent biblical passage (see Box 5.1).

Elijah accuses the Israelites of having forsaken the covenant, by which the Hebrew word *berit* is used, and that calls into question the integrity of Israel. Why does Elijah attend the rite of circumcision of every Jewish baby boy? A story in a medieval collection answers that question.

The Israelites were wont to circumcise until they were divided into two kingdoms. The kingdom of Ephraim cast off from themselves the covenant of circumcision. Elijah, may he be remembered for good, arose and was zealous with a mighty passion, and he adjured the heavens to send down neither dew nor rain upon the earth. Jezebel heard about it and sought to slay him.

Elijah arose and prayed before the Holy One, blessed be he. The Holy One, blessed be he, said to him, "Are you better than your fathers (1 Kgs. 19:4)?" Esau sought to slay Jacob, but he fled before him, as it is said, "And Jacob fled into the field of Aram" (Hos. 12:12).

"Pharaoh sought to slay Moses, who fled before him and he was saved, as it is said, 'Now when Pharaoh heard this thing, he sought to slay Moses. And Moses fled from the face of Pharaoh' (Exod. 2:15)."

"Saul sought to slay David, who fled before him and was saved, as it is said, 'If you save not your life tonight, tomorrow you will be killed' (1 Sam. 19:11)."

Another text says, "And David fled and escaped" (1 Sam. 19:18).

Elijah, may he be remembered for good, arose and fled from the Land of Israel, and he betook himself to Mount Horeb, as it is said, "and he arose and ate and drank" (1 Kgs. 19:8).

BOX 5.1 THE BLESSING AFTER THE RITE OF CIRCUMCISION

Tosefta Berakhot 6:13

A. What does the one who recites a benediction [after the circumcision is performed] say?

B. [He says], ["Praised be Thou, O Lord ...] who sanctified the beloved [i.e., Isaac] from the womb and placed [the mark of] a statute in his flesh, and sealed his offspring with the sign of the holy covenant. As [our] reward for [having observed] this [commandment], O living God, our Portion and our Rock, now save the beloved of our flesh from destruction [i.e., let the wound heal and preserve the child's life]. Praised [be Thou, O Lord,] who establishes the covenant." He who circumcises proselytes says, "Praised be Thou, O Lord ... who has sanctified us through his commandments and commanded us to circumcise proselytes, to cause the blood of the covenant to flow from them, for were it not for the blood of the covenant, the heavens and earth would not exist, as it is written, *If I have not established my covenant with day and night and the ordinances of heaven and earth* (Jer. 33:25). Praised (be Thou, O Lord,) who establishes the covenant."

He who circumcises slaves says, "Praised (be Thou, O Lord ...) who has sanctified us through his commandments and commanded us concerning circumcision." The one who recites a benediction (after the circumcision is performed) says, "Praised (be Thou, O Lord) who has sanctified us through his commandments and commanded us to circumcise slaves and to cause the blood of the covenant to flow from them."

Then the Holy One, blessed be he, was revealed to him and said to him, "What are you doing here, Elijah?"
He answered him saying, "I have been very zealous."

The Holy One, blessed be he, said to him, "You are always zealous. You were zealous in Shittim on account of the immorality. For it is said, 'Phineas, the son of Eleazar, the son of Aaron the priest, turned my wrath away from the children of Israel, in that he was zealous with my zeal among them' (Num. 25:11).

"Here you are also zealous, By your life! They shall not observe the covenant of circumcision until you see it done with your own eyes."

Hence the sages have instituted the custom that people should have a seat of honor for the messenger of the covenant, for Elijah, may he be remembered for good, is called the messenger of the covenant, as it is said, And the messenger of the covenant, whom you delight in, behold he comes (Mal. 3:1).

(Friedlander 1916: 212–14)

So too the "messenger of the covenant (*berit*)" (Mal. 1:23) is the prophet Elijah, and he is present whenever a Jewish son enters the Covenant of Abraham, which is circumcision. God therefore ordered him to come to every circumcision so as to witness the loyalty of the Jews to the covenant. Elijah then serves as the guardian for the newborn, just as he raised the child of the widow from the dead (1 Kgs. 17:17–24). Along these same lines on the Seder table of Passover, a cup of wine is poured for Elijah, and the door is opened for Elijah to join in the rite.

Setting a seat for Elijah serves to invoke the presence of the guardian of the newborn and the zealous advocate of the rite of the circumcision of the covenant. Celebrating with the family of the newborn are not "all Israel" in general, but a very specific personage indeed. The gesture of setting the chair silent sets the stage for an event in the life of the family not of the child alone but of all Israel. The chair of Elijah, filled by the one who holds the child, sets the newborn baby into Elijah's lap. The enchantment extends through the furnishing of the room; what is not ordinarily present is introduced, and that makes all the difference.

We move, third, from gesture to formula, for before the rite itself, as the mohel takes the knife to cut the foreskin, these words are said as blessing:

Praised are You ... who sanctified us with Your commandments and commanded us to bring the son into the Covenant of Abraham our father.

The explicit invocation of Abraham's covenant turns the concrete action in the here and now into a simile of the paradigm and archetype: The individual Israelite says, "I circumcise my son just as Abraham circumcised Isaac at eight days, and Ishmael. What I do is like what he did. Things are more than what they seem. Then I am a father, like Abraham, and – more to the point – my fatherhood is like Abraham's."

The operation done, fourth, the wine is blessed, introducing yet a further occasion of enchantment (see Box 5.1). The covenant is not a generality; it is specific, concrete, fleshly. It is, moreover, meant to accomplish a very specific goal – as all religion means to attain concrete purposes – and that is to secure a place for the child, a blessing for the child. By virtue of the rite, the child enters the covenant, meaning that he joins that unseen "Israel" that through blood enters an agreement with God. Then the blessing of the covenant is owing to the child. For covenants or contracts cut both ways.

After the father has recited the blessing, "who has sanctified us by his commandments and has commanded us to induct him into the covenant of our father, Abraham," the community responds: "just as he has entered the covenant, so may he be introduced to Torah, the *huppah* [marriage canopy] and good deeds." Schachter interprets those who are present as follows:

> In the presence of Elijah ... Torah – as against idolatry; in the presence of Phineas ... huppah, as against sexual licentiousness; in the presence of Abraham ... to good deeds: For I have singled him out that he may instruct his children and his posterity to keep the way of the Lord by doing what is just and right (Gen. 18:18).
>
> (Schachter 1986: 41)

The words evoke the scene, Elijah complaining to God, Abraham obediently circumcising his sons, Phineas, calming God's wrath by an act of violence, with whom a covenant of peace then is made.

HOW THE GRACE AFTER MEALS SITUATES THE ISRAELITE WITHIN THE NARRATIVES OF JUDAISM

At the end of any meal at which bread is eaten, the Grace after Meals takes what has happened – people were hungry, so they ate bread – and in that context treats God's provision of nourishment as a foretaste of the recovery of the Land and the restoration of Zion. A meal is a this-worldly experience of salvation, redemption in the end of days. The great theological constructions, Creation, Revelation, Redemption, are woven together in the response to eating a meal. To understand the setting, we recall that in classical Judaism, the table at which meals are eaten is regarded as the equivalent of the sacred altar in the temple. The washing of hands before eating bread means that each Jew before eating had to attain the state of ritual purity like the priest in the sacred act of making a sacrifice.

On Sabbaths and festivals – moments of eternity in time – the assembled Israelites first sing Psalm 126:

> When the Lord brought back those that returned to Zion, we were like dreamers. Our mouth was filled with laughter, our tongue with singing. Restore our fortunes, O Lord, as the streams in the dry land. They that sow in tears shall reap in joy.

It would be hard to miss the point: The meal is now treated as the realization in the here and now of the restoration to the Land. Then comes the recitation of the Grace after Meals. It follows the outline: Thanks for the food itself, thanks for the land that produces the food, supplication for restoration of Israel to the Land, the rebuilding of Jerusalem and the renewal of the temple offerings of atonement:

> Blessed art Thou, Lord our God, King of the Universe, who nourishes all the world by His goodness, in grace, in mercy, and in compassion: He gives bread to all flesh, for His mercy is everlasting. And because of His great goodness we have never lacked, and so may we never lack, sustenance – for the sake of His great Name. For He nourishes and feeds everyone, is good to all, and provides food for each one of the creatures He created.
>
> Blessed art Thou, O Lord, who feeds everyone.
>
> We thank Thee, Lord our God, for having given our fathers as a heritage a pleasant, a good and spacious land; for having taken us out of the land of Egypt, for having redeemed us from the house of bondage; for Thy covenant, which Thou hast set as a seal in our flesh,

for Thy Torah which Thou has taught us, for Thy statutes which Thou hast made known to us, for the life of grace and mercy Thou hast graciously bestowed upon us, and for the nourishment with which Thou dost nourish us and feed us always, every day, in every season, and every hour.

For all these things, Lord our God, we thank and praise Thee; may Thy praises continually be in the mouth of every living thing, as it is written, And thou shalt eat and be satisfied, and bless the Lord thy God for the good Land which He hath given thee.

Blessed art Thou, O Lord, for the Land and its food.

O Lord our God, have pity on Thy people Israel, on Thy city Jerusalem, on Zion the place of Thy glory, on the royal house of David Thy Messiah, and on the great and holy house which is called by Thy Name. Our God, our Father, feed us and speed us, nourish us and make us flourish, unstintingly, O Lord our God, speedily free us from all distress.

And let us not, O Lord our God, find ourselves in need of gifts from flesh and blood, or of a loan from anyone save from Thy full, generous, abundant, wide-open hand; so we may never be humiliated, or put to shame.

O rebuild Jerusalem, the holy city, speedily in our day. Blessed art Thou, Lord, who in mercy will rebuild Jerusalem. Amen.

Blessed art Thou, Lord our God, King of the Universe, Thou God, who art our Father, our powerful king, our creator and redeemer, who made us, our holy one, the holy one of Jacob, our shepherd, shepherd of Israel, the good king, who visits His goodness upon all; for every single day He has brought good, He does bring good, He will bring good upon us; He has rewarded us, does regard, and will always reward us, with grace, mercy and compassion, amplitude, deliverance and prosperity, blessing and salvation, comfort, and a living, sustenance, pity and peace, and all good – let us not want any manner of good whatever.

(Goldin 1955: 9, 15–16)

The implicit narrative is familiar: The Promised Land and its blessings. The Promised Land lay at the end of redemption from Egyptian bondage. Holding it, enjoying it – these form a sign that the covenant is intact and in force and that Israel is loyal to its part of the contract and God to his. The Promised Land, the Exodus, the covenant – these all depend upon the Torah, statutes, and a life of grace and mercy, here embodied in and evoked by the nourishment of the meal. Thanksgiving wells up, and the paragraph ends with praises for the Land and its food.

Then the chief theme recurs – that is, redemption and hope for return, and then future prosperity in the Land: "May God pity the people, the city, Zion, the royal house of the Messiah, the Holy Temple." The nourishment of this meal is but a foretaste of the nourishment of the messianic time, just as the joy of the wedding is a foretaste of the messianic rejoicing.

Still, it is not the messianic time, so Israel finally asks not to depend upon the gifts or mortal men but only upon those of the generous, wide-open hand of God. And then "rebuild Jerusalem." The concluding paragraph summarizes the whole, giving thanks for creation, redemption, divine goodness, every blessing. So the physical experience of hunger assuaged by eating a meal is transformed into an acting out of the narrative, which takes over and enchants everyday life. Indeed, religion is story – what else can it ever have been? The law of Judaism answers that question.

PART II

JUDAISM IN BEHAVIOR AND BELIEF

6

THE PURPOSE OF THE LAW, THE TEN COMMANDMENTS, THE SABBATH

Actions act out the worldview and the way of life of Judaism. These actions are called *mitzvot*, commandments, and in carrying them out, the faithful Israelite is made holy and takes a place in the Kingdom of God, subjecting himself or herself to God's rule. The blessing before carrying out a commandment transforms a secular into a religious action. The formula is, "Blessed are you, Lord our God, who has sanctified us by his commandments and commanded us to ... " do such and so.

The purpose of the commandments is to realize the teaching of prophecy, "The righteous shall live by his faith" (Hab. 2:4) (see Box 6.1). Living by faith is thus defined as acting out the faith, or worldview, in concrete deeds, or way of life.

The Ten Commandments lay down the basic principles of the holy way of life. The Sabbath, celebrating Creation and the Exodus from Egypt, is fully realized in commandments of repose and refraining from servile labor. The Sabbath thus realizes the condition of Creation at the end of the six days of labor and the moment when God sanctified creation and rested on the seventh day.

BOX 6.1 "THE RIGHTEOUS SHALL LIVE BY HIS FAITH"

Among many efforts at summarizing life under the law of the Torah, the most comprehensive is attributed to R. Simelai, in the following composition:

Talmud of Babylonia Makkot 23b–24a / 3:16 II.1

R. Simelai expounded, "Six hundred and thirteen command-ments were given to Moses, three hundred and sixty-five negative ones, corresponding to the number of the days of the solar year, and two hundred forty-eight positive command-ments, corresponding to the parts of man's body.

"David came and reduced them to eleven: 'A Psalm of David: Lord, who shall sojourn in thy tabernacle, and who shall dwell in thy holy mountain? (i) He who walks uprightly and (ii) works righteousness and (iii) speaks truth in his heart and (iv) has no slander on his tongue and (v) does no evil to his fellow and (vi) does not take up a reproach against his neighbor, (vii) in whose eyes a vile person is despised but (viii) honors those who fear the Lord. (ix) He swears to his own hurt and changes not. (x) He does not lend on interest. (xi) He does not take a bribe against the innocent' (Ps. 15).

"Isaiah came and reduced them to six: '(i) He who walks righteously and (ii) speaks uprightly, (iii) he who despises the gain of oppressions, (iv) shakes his hand from holding bribes, (v) stops his ear from hearing of blood, (vi) and shuts his eyes from looking upon evil, he shall dwell on high' (Isa. 33:25–26).

"Micah came and reduced them to three: 'It has been told you, man, what is good, and what the Lord demands from you, (i) only to do justly and (ii) to love mercy, and (iii) to walk humbly before God' (Mic. 6:8)."

'only to do justly': this refers to justice.

'to love mercy': this refers to doing acts of loving kindness.

'to walk humbly before God': this refers to accompanying a corpse to the grave and welcoming the bride.

"And does this not yield a conclusion a fortiori: If matters that are not ordinarily done in private are referred to by the Torah as 'walking humbly before God,' all the more so matters that ordinarily are done in private.

"Isaiah again came and reduced them to two: 'Thus says the Lord, (i) Keep justice and (ii) do righteousness' (Isa. 56:1).

"Amos came and reduced them to a single one, as it is said, 'For thus says the Lord to the house of Israel. Seek Me and live.'

"Habakkuk further came and based them on one, as it is said, 'But the righteous shall live by his faith' (Hab. 2:4)."

The Talmudic rabbis here try to define the point of the myriad of religious obligations of which the Torah is comprised. The way of life embodies the worldview, and the worldview explains the way of life. But at the heart of matters is the definition of the Israelite and his or her purpose in life. While many of the commandments concern matters we regard as ritual, fasting on the Day of Atonement, for example, the great sages insist that the heart of the matter concerns moral and ethical conduct. And these come to their climax in the attitude of the Israelite: Faith in God, integrity in walking humbly with Him.

THE 613 COMMANDMENTS AND THEIR SINGLE PURPOSE

Basic to Judaism are the commandments (*mitzvot*), which act out the Judaic worldview and way of life. The commandments are grouped. People speak of 613 commandments, the Ten Commandments, and commandments concerning particular topics, such as the Sabbath and its commandment to rest and cease from creative labor. The commandments, when enumerated at 613, involve 365 matching the days of the solar year and 248 corresponding to the number of bones of the body. The commandments of action or refraining from action govern everyday life and transactions, both social and personal.

These commandments may concern theological convictions. "You shall love the Lord your God with all your heart, with all your soul, and with all your might" (Deut. 6:4) is a principal among these. They may encompass ethical obligations. "What is hateful to yourself do not do to your fellow," represents that group. They may concern matters of ritual, refraining from forbidden foods for example. That is because Judaism knows no distinction between right and rite, between theology and law. Rather, it treats each as the realization of the other and its fulfillment. The entire way of life and worldview embody Israel's covenant with God. At hand is a system of covenantal nomism, meaning laws carried out in a covenanted relationship with God.

What is the point of the covenant? The Torah not only commands Israel "you shall be holy, for I the Lord your God am holy" (Lev. 19:2), it defines holiness through the performance of religious duties, which are many. At the same time, the Torah offers general rules of sanctification of the community of Israel, for example, "You shall love your neighbor as yourself" (Lev. 19:18). Accordingly, the master narrative of Judaism at its foundations describes in vast detail the rules for living in God's kingdom under the yoke of the Torah.

Through myriads of details, it is, then, easy to lose sight of the purpose of the whole. Hence, as Moses did in Leviticus 19:2 and 19:18, so too the rabbinic sages made every effort at teaching the purpose of the laws of the Torah, finding the main point realized in the details. In a series of stories and sayings, they declared what they deemed to form the heart and soul, the center of the system as a whole (see Box 6.1).

"'WHAT IS HATEFUL TO YOU, TO YOUR FELLOW DON'T DO.' THAT'S THE ENTIRETY OF THE TORAH; EVERYTHING ELSE IS ELABORATION. SO GO, STUDY!"

Summarizing the formidable program of actions to be taken or to be refrained from defines the task of the great masters of the Torah. The single most famous such statement of "the whole Torah" derives from Hillel, the first-century C.E. Pharisaic authority:

Talmud of Babylonia tractate Shabbat 30b–31a / 2:5 I.12

There was another case of a gentile who came before Shammai. He said to him, "Convert me on the stipulation that you teach me the entire Torah while I am standing on one foot." He drove him off with the building cubit that he had in his hand.

He came before Hillel: "Convert me."

He said to him, "'What is hateful to you, to your fellow don't do.' That's the entirety of the Torah; everything else is elaboration. So go, study."

This famous saying frequently is cited only in part, the part that amplifies Leviticus 19:18: "Love your neighbor as yourself." The climax about elaboration and Torah study is often left out. That makes matters easier than they are intended to be. But, we see, Torah study is integral to life under the law of the Torah, and ignorance is the enemy of piety.

"STUDY IS GREATER, FOR STUDY BRINGS ABOUT ACTION"

Everything else is elaboration. So go, study. Then which is more important, doing the deed or studying about it in the Torah? That question is answered in so many words:

Talmud of Babylonia Qiddushin 1:10E–G I.2/22a

Once R. Tarfon and the elders were reclining at a banquet in the upper room of the house of Nitseh in Lud. This question was raised for them: "Is study greater or is action greater?"

R. Tarfon responded: "Action is greater."

R. Aqiba responded: "Study is greater."

All responded, saying, "Study is greater, for study brings about action."

So the system is integrated, making the same statement in diverse ways. Now the point of the way of life set forth by the law of the Torah is studying the Torah so as to keep the commandments. The value of study depends on the doing of the deed. The matter is resolved by Eleazar b. Azariah in this language:

Tractate Abot 3:17

R. Eleazar b. Azariah says, "If there is no learning of Torah, there is no proper conduct.

"If there is no proper conduct, there is no learning in Torah."

He would say, "Anyone whose wisdom is greater than his deeds – to what is he to be likened? To a tree with abundant foliage, but few roots.

"When the winds come, they will uproot it and blow it down,

"as it is said, 'He shall be like a tamarisk in the desert and shall not see when good comes but shall inhabit the parched places in the wilderness' (Jer. 17:6).

"But anyone whose deeds are greater than his wisdom – to what is he to be likened? To a tree with little foliage but abundant roots.

"For even if all the winds in the world were to come and blast at it, they will not move it from its place,

"as it is said, 'He shall be as a tree planted by the waters, and that spreads out its roots by the river, and shall not fear when heat comes, and his leaf shall be green, and shall not be careful in the year of drought, neither shall cease from yielding fruit' (Jer. 17: 8)."

Basic to Judaism, then, is the perpetual presence of God, and the life of Judaism requires constant awareness of God's concern for the actions and attitudes of every individual. The picture we gain of life under the law of the Torah is a life focused on God's concerns, a life meant to respond to the expression of God's love for Israel that is embodied in the Torah. Above all, we see an insistent effort on classifying religious requirements as less or as more important, depending on the sense of proportion and purpose that animates the law as a whole.

But that is not the view of Judaism that its critics have formed, whether Jesus in his arguments with the Pharisees, or the contemporary secular or Reform critics of classical Judaism in their rejection of the law. A cultural bias comes into play as a result of millennia of criticism of people who "care more for what goes into their mouths" – kosher food – "than for what comes out" – gossip and slander. The sages understood full well that some commandments are more important than others, for example, that the religious duty of saving a life takes priority even over the observance of the Sabbath.

Still, when people think of law, they ordinarily imagine a religion for bookkeepers, who tote up the good deeds and debit the bad and call the result salvation or damnation, depending on the outcome. But life under the Torah brings the joy of expressing love of God through a cycle of celebration.

THE TEN COMMANDMENTS

The Ten Commandments occur at two passages, Exodus 20:1–17 and Deuteronomy 5:6–21. They are basic to Judaism and exhibit that insistence on the cogency of theology and law, ethics and ritual, right and rite that characterizes Judaism as a whole.

Here, at the centerpiece of the covenant, stand the Ten Commandments. For the Ten Commandments are not ten different things. They are one thing in ten forms: "I am the Lord your God ... therefore, don't do this, and do that." The Ten Commandments are the details, the "I am the Lord your God" is the main thing. So the Ten Commandments outline a path to follow to make God "your God." And to leave that Egypt that "the Lord your God" helps you escape slavery in one form or another.

We noted that to live the life of Judaism is to recognize at all times God's love for us and concern for our actions and attitudes. How do the Ten Commandments define the Israelite's relationship with God? The very order of matters answers. God begins by announcing that Israel is to have only the Lord for God. Why start there? Because before one can agree to the details, one has to adopt the main point. God rules, and Israel accepts God's dominion. On the basis of that fact, all else follows.

This point is made explicit in several ways. First of all, Israel has to affirm that it has already accepted God's rule, in which case it is instructed in the first detail of that rule, which is not to have other gods.

Mekhilta attributed to R. Ishmael LI.I.1 Bahodesh 5

"You shall have no other gods before me" (Exod. 20:3):

Why is this stated?

Since it says, "I am the Lord your God."

The matter may be compared to the case of a mortal king who came to a town. His staff said to him, "Issue decrees for them."

He said to them, "No. When they have accepted my dominion, then I shall issue decrees over them. For if they do not accept my dominion, how are they going to carry out my decrees?"

So said the Omnipresent to Israel, "I am the Lord your God.

"You shall have no other gods before me.

"I am the one whose dominion you accepted upon yourselves in Egypt."

They said to him, "Indeed so."

"And just as you accepted my dominion upon yourself, now likewise accept my decrees: 'You shall have no other gods before me.'"

The Ten Commandments speak not in generalities but require careful and explicit application to all manner of situations: This is what it means, in the here and the now, to keep the Ten Commandments:

Mekhilta attributed to R. Ishmael LII.3 Bahodesh 6

"You shall not make for yourself a graven image":

One shall not make one that is engraved, but may one make one that is solid?

The Torah says, "or any likeness of anything."

One should not make a solid one, but may one plant a tree for oneself as an idol?

The Torah says, "You shall not plant an Asherah for yourself" (Deut. 16:21).

One may not plant a tree for oneself as an idol, but perhaps one may make a tree into an idol?

The Torah says, "of any kind of tree."

One may not make an idol of a tree, but perhaps one may make one of a stone?

The Torah says, "Nor shall you place any figured stone."

One may not make an idol of stone, but perhaps one may make an idol of silver or gold?

The Torah says, "Gods of silver or gods of gold you shall not make for yourself."

One may not make an idol of silver or gold, but perhaps one may make one of copper, iron, tin, or lead?

The Torah says, "Nor make for yourselves molten gods" (Lev. 19:4).

One may not make for oneself any of these images.

But may one make an image of any figure?

The Torah says, "lest you deal corruptly and make for yourself a graven image, even the form of any figure" (Deut. 4:16).

One may not make an image of a figure, but perhaps one may make an image of cattle or fowl?

The Torah says, "The likeness of any beast that is on the earth, the likeness of any winged fowl" (Deut. 4:17).

One may not make an image of cattle or fowl, but perhaps he may make an image of fish, locusts, unclean animals, or reptiles?

The Torah says, "The likeness of any thing that creeps on the ground, the likeness of any fish that is in the water" (Deut. 4:18).

One shall not make an image of any of these, but perhaps one may make an image of the sun, moon, stars, or planets?

The Torah says, "lest you lift up your eyes to heaven" (Deut. 4:18).

One may not make an image of any of these, but perhaps one may make an image of angels, cherubim, or Ophannim?

The Torah says, "of anything that is in heaven."

Since the Torah says, "that is in heaven above, [or that is in the earth beneath, or that is in the water under the earth]," might one suppose that that involves only sun, moon, stars, or planets?

It says, "above," that is, not the image of angels, cherubim, or Ophannim.

One may not make an image of any of these, but perhaps one may make an image of deeps and darkness?

The Torah says, "or that is in the water under the earth."

We see a sustained and searching process, by which a general rule is made specific and shown to cover every conceivable situation. This is not a generalization, left up to our own imagination. It is a literal and uncompromising inquiry. Not having graven images is the generalization; everything else is the detail, and, again, God lives in the details.

Take the case now that concerns honor of parents. Here is how Judaism in detail understands the intent and rule of the Torah:

Mekhilta attributed to R. Ishmael LIV:I.1 Bahodesh 8.1–2

"Honor your father and your mother [that your days may be long in the land which the Lord your God gives you]":

Might I infer that this is with words?

The Torah says, "Honor the Lord with your substance" (Prov. 3:9).

That means, with food, drink, and fresh garments ...

Rabbi says, "Precious before the One who spoke and brought the world into being is the honor owing to father and mother, "for he has declared equal the honor owing to them and the honor owing to him, the fear owing to them and the fear owing to him, curing them and cursing him.

"It is written: 'Honor your father and your mother,' and as a counterpart: 'Honor the Lord with your substance' (Prov. 3:9).

"The Torah thus has declared equal the honor owing to them and the honor owing to him.

"'You shall fear every man his mother and his father' (Lev. 19:3), and, as a counterpart: 'You shall fear the Lord your God' (Deut. 6:13).

"The Torah thus has declared equal the fear owing to them and the fear owing to him.

"'And he who curses his father or his mother shall surely be put to death' (Exod. 21:17), and correspondingly: 'Whoever curses his God' (Lev. 24:15).

"The Torah thus has declared equal the cursing them and cursing him."

[Rabbi continues,] "Come and note that the reward [for obeying the two commandments is the same].

"'Honor the Lord with your substance ... so shall your barns be filled with plenty' (Prov. 3:9–10), and 'Honor your father and your mother that your days may be long in the land which the Lord your God gives you.'

"'You shall fear the Lord your God' (Deut. 6:13), as a reward: 'But to you that fear my name shall the sun of righteousness arise with healing in its wings' (Mal. 3:20).

"'You shall fear every man his mother and his father and you shall keep my Sabbaths' (Lev. 19:3).

"And as a reward? 'If you turn away your foot because of the Sabbath, then you shall delight yourself in the Lord' (Isa. 58:13–14)."

Rabbi says, "It is perfectly self-evident before the One who spoke and brought the world into being that a person honors the mother more than the father, because she brings him along with words. Therefore the Torah gave precedence to the father over the mother as to honor.

"And it is perfectly self-evident before the One who spoke and brought the world into being that a person fears his father more than the mother, because the father teaches him Torah. Therefore the Torah gave precedence to the mother over the father as to fear.

"In a case in which something is lacking, [the Torah] thereby made it whole.

"But might one suppose that whoever takes precedence in the Torah takes precedence in deed?

"The Torah says, 'You shall fear every man his mother and his father' (Lev. 19:3),

"indicating that both of them are equal to one another."

The Ten Commandments, consistent with the story of the creation of Adam and Eve, form the first feminist platform. Just as "in our image, after our likeness" means "male and female he made them," so here, honoring parents means mother and father, not just love of mother and fear of father, but both, in perfect equality.

The whole holds together if we look for points in common and correspondences. People familiar with the symbols of Judaism will know that the Ten Commandments are set forth in two groups of five, facing one another. So there are correspondences between the commandments. If you do one, the other follows. Violate one, the other is broken as well. When we recognize these correspondences between each set of five commandments and the complementary ones, we grasp yet another layer of meaning in the Ten Commandments.

Mekhilta attributed to R. Ishmael LIV:III.1 Bahodesh 8

"How were the Ten Commandments set forth?

"There were five on one tablet, five on the other.

"On the one was written, 'I am the Lord your God,'

"and opposite it: 'You shall not murder.'

"The Torah thus indicates that whoever sheds blood is regarded as though he had diminished the divine image.

"The matter may be compared to the case of a mortal king who came into a town, and the people set up in his honor icons, and they made statues of him, and they minted coins in his honor.

"After a while they overturned his icons, broke his statues, and invalidated his coins, so diminishing the image of the king.

"Thus whoever sheds blood is regarded as though he had diminished the divine image, for it is said, 'Whoever sheds man's blood ... for in the image of God he made man' (Gen. 9:6)."

The whole of the Torah's picture of humankind is going to emerge in the Ten Commandments. We recall how the Torah insists that we are in God's image and likeness, and that means we look like God. Then murder diminishes God's image too. So much for murder and God's image. Along these same lines, adultery represents a denial of God:

> "On the one was written, 'You shall have no other god'
> "and opposite it: 'You shall not commit adultery.'
> "The Torah thus indicates that whoever worships an idol is regarded as though he had committed adultery against the Omnipresent, for it is said, 'You wife that commits adultery, that takes strangers instead of your husband' (Ezek. 16:32); 'And the Lord said to me, Go yet, love a woman beloved of her friend and an adulteress' (Hos. 3:1)."

Taking God's name in vain is the result of thievery. People often take oaths, so Judaism notes, in connection with the claim that they have not taken someone else's property. Hence the correspondence:

> "On the one was written, 'You shall not take the name of the Lord your God in vain,'
> "and opposite it: 'You shall not steal.'
> "The Torah thus indicates that whoever steals in the end will end up taking a false oath: 'Will you steal, murder, commit adultery, and swear falsely' (Jer. 7:9); 'Swearing and lying, killing and stealing, and committing adultery' (Hos. 4:2)."

What about the Sabbath? That is surely a commandment that has no counterpart, since it is (so it is seen by outsiders) a matter of pure "ritual," without ethical or moral implications. But the Sabbath stands for Creation and celebrates God's creating the world. There is nothing less narrowly ritualistic than the Sabbath, given its sense and meaning:

> "On the one was written, 'Remember the Sabbath day to keep it holy,'
> "and opposite it: 'You shall not bear false witness.'
> "The Torah thus indicates that whoever violates the Sabbath is as though he had given testimony before the One who spoke and

> brought the world into being, indicating that he had not created his world in six days and not rested on the seventh, and whoever keeps the Sabbath day is as though he had given testimony before the One who spoke and brought the world into being, indicating that he had created his world in six days and rested on the seventh: 'For you are my witnesses, says the Lord' (Isa. 43:10)."

Is there a reward and punishment contained within the correspondences? So our sages maintain:

> "On the one was written, 'Honor your father and your mother,'
> "and opposite it: 'You shall not covet your neighbor's wife.'
> "The Torah thus indicates that whoever covets in the end will produce a son who curses his father and honors one who is not his father.
> Thus the Ten Commandments were given, five on this tablet, and five on that," the words of R. Hananiah b. Gamaliel.

What Hananiah has done, we now realize, is to discover many of the basic principles of Judaism, that is, of the Torah, in these Ten Commandments.

THE SABBATH

The sanctification of the seventh day as the Sabbath takes a primary role in the Judaic way of life. Basic to all Judaic theology and law is the Sabbath, one of the Ten Commandments. It is the day of rest that (in Exodus) commemorates the sanctification of creation at the end of the six days of work that brought the world into being, and that further (in Deuteronomy) commemorates the slavery of the Israelites in Egypt and secures repose for man and beast alike.

The double meaning – creation in the version of the Ten Commandments given in Exodus, liberation in the counterpart in Deuteronomy – hardly explains the centrality of the Sabbath in classical Judaism. What is the conviction of Judaism that God cherishes Israel's repose, that Israel offers God its repose in celebration of creation? Like God in the creation narrative of Genesis 1:1–2:4, Israel rests on the seventh day. Like a mother, God cares about

Israel's mental and physical health: Get enough rest, and the right kind of rest. One's own good health is a person's best offering to God.

To the Sabbath-observing Israelite, the Sabbath is the chief sign of God's grace: "For thou hast chosen us and sanctified us above all nations, in love and favor has given us thy holy Sabbath as an inheritance." So states the Sanctification of the Sabbath wine. Likewise in the Sabbath morning liturgy,

> You did not give it [Sabbath] to the nations of the earth, nor did you make it the heritage of idolaters, nor in its rest will unrighteous men find a place.
> But to Israel your people you have given it in love, to the seed of Jacob whom you have chosen, to that people who sanctify the Sabbath day. All of them find fulfillment and joy from your bounty.
> For the seventh day did you choose and sanctify as the most pleasant of days and you called it a memorial to the works of creation.

Here again we find a profusion of themes, this time centered upon the Sabbath. The Sabbath is a sign of the covenant. It is a gift of grace, which neither idolaters nor evil people may enjoy. It is the testimony of the chosenness of Israel. And it is the most pleasant of days. Keeping the Sabbath is living in God's kingdom: "Those who keep the Sabbath and call it a delight will rejoice in your kingdom." So states the additional Sabbath prayer. Keeping the Sabbath now is a foretaste of the redemption: "This day is for Israel light and rejoicing." The rest of the Sabbath is, as the afternoon prayer affirms, "a rest granted in generous love, a true and faithful rest ... Let your children realize that their rest is from you, and by their rest may they sanctify your name."

The word Sabbath simply renders the Hebrew *Shabbat*; it does not translate it, for there is no translation. In no other tradition or culture can an equivalent word be found. The Sabbath restores the perfection of Eden, when God blessed and sanctified creation as perfect, and all things were at rest – where and how they should be. When Israel recreates the situation of the perfect Sabbath, the Messiah will come. Indeed, it is the restoration of Eden that defines the Messiah's task, so Israel has in its power the perfection of the world.

Yerushalmi Taanit 1:1 II.5

Said R Levi, "If Israel should keep a single Sabbath in the proper way, forthwith the son of David will come.

"What is the scriptural basis for this view? 'Moses said, "Eat it today, for today is a Sabbath to the Lord; [today you will not find it in the field]"' (Exod. 16:25).

"And it says, '[For thus said the Lord God, the Holy One of Israel] In returning and rest you shall be saved; [in quietness and in trust shall be your strength.' And you would not]" (Isa. 30:15).

"By means of returning and [Sabbath] rest you will be redeemed."

The Sabbath captures the essence of the Judaic way of life and worldview, the union of belief and behavior, conduct and conviction, all in the project of transforming Israel into the kingdom of priests and the holy people, the Israelite into the human being in God's image, after God's likeness.

So much for the behavior that is basic to Judaism. What about the basic beliefs of that religion, beginning with belief in one unique God of all the world, made known in the Torah and in nature?

7

GOD IS ONE, MERCIFUL AND JUST

The worldview of Judaism spells out belief in one God, creator of heaven and earth, who is just and merciful. God is made known in as many ways as there are types of people in the world, but it is always one and the same God, ruling the world in a consistent way by rational rules. That theology is called "ethical monotheism," the belief that God is all-powerful and bound by the same rules of justice and ethics that apply to humanity. The creed of Judaism, recited in worship morning and night, presents the one and only God as creator of the world, revealer of the Torah, and redeemer of Israel.

Unique to ethical monotheism is the problem of evil: Why do bad things happen to good people, and good things to bad? Because God is all-powerful and ethical, people ask where is justice and why there is evil. Judaism solves that problem. It maintains that the story of a life does not end at the grave. For after death, in the end of days, the dead will rise from their graves. This is called "the Resurrection of the Dead." Then comes a last judgment, when God rewards with eternal life and bliss those who lived lives of justice and mercy and punishes with ultimate extinction those who lived wickedly. So God ultimately rights all wrongs, and humanity will know God's mercy and justice in the end. Belief in the Resurrection of the Dead and the Last Judgment is as basic to Judaism's world-view as the belief in one transcendent God.

ETHICAL MONOTHEISM

The basic belief of Judaism is that God is One, merciful and just and shows his traits of unity, mercy, and justice in his dominion over creation. By that statement, Judaism means God is the one and only God; God is unique, and there is no other. He is responsible for all that is, for all that happens. And nothing is arbitrary.

Judaism's worldview is that of ethical monotheism. Monotheism is the doctrine that there is one God alone, possessing the power to do all things. Polytheism, the opposite of monotheism, is the doctrine that there are many gods, each empowered to take charge of a given task. Monotheism is made ethical by the belief that the one God is bound by the same laws of right and wrong, good and evil, that govern humanity. In polytheism some gods are benevolent, some not.

The upshot is monotheism explains many things in one way, by attributing all that happens to the will of the one God. Polytheism explains one thing in many ways, by crediting what happens to the intervention of competing gods. And monotheism knows God as benevolent and loving, while in polytheism some gods are, and some are not, moved by good will.

Ethical monotheism is not a philosophical proposition of an abstract character, but a statement of the facts of concrete experience. Israelites know God through his acts in their history, acts of punishment for sin and rebellion but also acts of redemption and salvation. While philosophers may offer proofs for the existence of God based on logic, Israelites know God in the Torah's story of what has happened to them by reason of his presence. The one God, accordingly, is made known in the Torah, which contains the record of God's activities on earth. For his part, God knows humanity through prayer and acts of merit, when people turn to him for favor and goodness. God's response to prayer and acts of merit is perceived by Israelites in everyday affairs.

God loves humanity, his creation, and craves their love in return. That is shown by the Shema, the creed that proclaims God's unity. Immediately follows is the commandment, "You shall love the Lord your God with all your heart, with all your soul, with all your might." The commandment to love God attests to God's love for his creatures: He commands what is beyond all imperatives, the gift of the heart, which can only be voluntary.

GOD REPRESENTED AS ONE

The main point is that God is made known in as many ways as there are types of people in the world, but it is always one and the same God, ruling the world in a consistent way by rational rules, which are cogent and made manifest in what happens. Here is how the diverse encounters with one and the same God are described in a classic rabbinic writing of the sixth century C.E.:

Pesiqta deRab Kahana XII:XXIV.6

A. Because the Holy One, blessed be he, had appeared to them at the sea like a heroic soldier, doing battle, appeared to them at Sinai like a teacher, teaching the repetition [of traditions], appeared to them in the time of Daniel like a sage, teaching Torah, appeared to them in the time of Solomon like a lover ...

The passage opens with an allusion to the incarnate forms taken by God, the representation of God as teacher, warrior, lover (of the congregation of Israel, it is, of course, understood).

B. [It was necessary for] the Holy One, blessed be he, to say to them, "You see me in many forms. But I am the same one who was at the sea, I am the same one who was at Sinai, I [anokhi] am the Lord your God who brought you out of the land of Egypt" (Exod. 20:2).

The qualification of the foregoing yields no difficulty. God appears in diverse models of incarnation. It is one and the same God. We come now to a restatement of the same matter:

A. Said R. Hiyya the Elder, "It is because through every manner of deed and every condition he had appeared to them [that he made that statement, namely:]

B. "he had appeared to them at the sea as a heroic soldier, carrying out battles in behalf of Israel,

C. "he had appeared to them at Sinai in the form of a teacher who was teaching Torah and standing in awe,

D. "he had appeared to them in the time of Daniel as an elder, teaching Torah, for it is appropriate for Torah to go forth from the mouth of sages,

E. "he had appeared to them in the time of Solomon as a youth, in accord with the practices of that generation: 'His aspect is like Lebanon, young as the cedars' (S. of S. 5:15),

F. "so at Sinai he appeared to them as a teacher, teaching Torah: 'I am the Lord your God who brought you out of the land of Egypt'" (Exod. 20:2).

When portrayed as a warrior, teacher, sage, and lover, God is represented in incarnate form, but it is always one and the same unique God.

THE CREED OF JUDAISM: "HEAR, O ISRAEL, THE LORD OUR GOD, THE LORD IS ONE"

The prayers recited morning and night proclaim the creed of Judaism, the Shema, which means "Hear," as in "Hear, O Israel, the Lord our God, the Lord is one." The recital of the Shema is introduced by a celebration of God as Creator of the world (see Box 7.1). A further preliminary statement celebrates God for revealing the Torah. Then comes the proclamation of God's unity. That is followed by the celebration of God as redeemer of Israel.

GOD AS CREATOR

Whatever happens in nature gives testimony to the unity and sovereignty of the Creator. And that testimony is not in unnatural disasters, but in the most ordinary events: Sunrise and sunset.

BOX 7.1 GOD AS CREATOR OF THE WORLD, CELEBRATED IN THE RECITATION OF THE SHEMA

In the morning, one says the following prayer before declaring the Shema:

Praised are You, O Lord our God, King of the universe.
You fix the cycles of light and darkness;
You ordain the order of all creation
You cause light to shine over the earth;
Your radiant mercy is upon its inhabitants.
In Your goodness the work of creation
Is continually renewed day by day ...
O cause a new light to shine on Zion;
May we all soon be worthy to behold its radiance.
Praised are You, O Lord, Creator of the heavenly bodies.

(Hadas 1966: 42)

These, especially, evoke the religious response to set the stage for what follows.

GOD REVEALS THE TORAH

For the faithful Israelite God is not merely Creator, but revealer, the mark of the purpose of the purposeful Creator. The works of creation serve to justify and to testify to the Torah, the revelation of Sinai. The Torah is the mark not merely of divine sovereignty, but of divine grace and love, source of life here and now and in eternity. Here is the way in which revelation takes concrete and specific form in the Judaic tradition: God, the Creator, revealed his will for creation through the Torah, given to Israel his people. That Torah contains the "laws of life" (see Box 7.2).

THE SHEMA ITSELF

Then in the recitation of the creed that forms the heart of the liturgy of Judaism comes the proclamation of the faith of Israel, "Hear O

BOX 7.2 GOD REVEALS THE TORAH

The second blessing recited before the proclamation of the
Shema, after the one concerning sunrise and sunset, celebrates
God's revelation of the Torah.

> Deep is Your love for us, O Lord our God;
> Bounteous is Your compassion and tenderness.
> You taught our fathers the laws of life,
> And they trusted in You, Father and king,
> For their sake be gracious to us, and teach us,
> That we may learn Your laws and trust in You.
> Father, merciful Father, have compassion upon us:
> Endow us with discernment and understanding.
> Grant us the will to study Your Torah,
> To heed its words and to teach its precepts ...
> Enlighten our eyes in Your Torah,
> Open our hearts to Your commandments ...
> Unite our thoughts with singleness of purpose
> To hold You in reverence and in love ...
> You have drawn us close to You;
> We praise You and thank You in truth.
> With love do we thankfully proclaim Your unity.
> And praise You who chose Your people Israel in love.

(Hadas 1966: 45 – 6)

Israel, the Lord our God, the Lord is One." This declaration represents
accepting the yoke of the Kingdom of God upon oneself. It means one
accepts God's rule in his or her life. A benediction follows: "Blessed be
the Name of his glorious Kingdom forever and ever." This declaration
represents accepting the yoke of the commandments, the resolve to
carry out religious obligations of commission and omission. So in
reciting the Shema, the Israelite by an act of will enters the
Kingdom of God and accepts God's rule on earth, in everyday life.

This proclamation, by which the pious person enters the
dominion of God and in attitude and action accepts God's rule, is
followed by three Scriptural passages. The first is Deuteronomy

6:5–9: "You shall love the Lord your God with all your heart, with all your soul, with all your might." And further, one must diligently teach one's children these words and talk of them everywhere and always, and place them on one's forehead, doorposts, and gates.

The second set of verses of Scripture is Deuteronomy 11:13–21, which emphasizes that if Jews keep the commandments, they will enjoy worldly blessings; but that if they do not, they will be punished and disappear from the good land God gives them.

The third is Numbers 15:37–41, the commandment to wear fringes on the corners of one's garments. The fringes are, today, attached to the prayer shawl worn at morning services by Conservative and some Reform Jews and worn on a separate undergarment for that purpose by Orthodox Jews, and they remind the faithful Israelite of *all* the commandments of the Lord.

GOD REDEEMS ISRAEL

After the recitation of the three paragraphs of the Shema comes the exposition of the doctrine that God saves Israel. This is illustrated by the Exodus from Egypt (see Box 7.3).

Redemption is both in the past and in the future. That God not only creates but also redeems is attested by the redemption from Egyptian bondage. The congregation repeats the exultant song of Moses and the people at the Red Sea, participants in a narrative drama, one that concerns the story of the salvation of old and of time to come. Then the people turn to the future and ask that Israel once more be redeemed. So much for the liturgical evocation of God's unity in creation, revelation, and redemption.

HOW DOES THE TORAH PROVE THE JUSTICE OF GOD?

When God judges and sentences, not only is the judgment fair but the penalty fits the crime with frightening precision. But so too, when God judges and awards a decision of merit, the reward proves equally exact. These two together, "measure for measure," the match of sin and penalty, meritorious deed and reward, then are shown to explain the point and purpose of one detail after another, and, all together, they add up to the portrait of a world order that is

BOX 7.3   GOD AS REDEEMER OF ISRAEL

In the end, it is the theme of God, not as Creator or Revealer, but God as Redeemer that concludes the twice-daily drama. The prayer after the declamation of the Shema is as follows:

> You are our King and our father's King,
> Our redeemer and our father's redeemer.
> You are our creator ...
> You have ever been our redeemer and deliverer
> There can be no God but You ...
> You, O Lord our God, rescued us from Egypt;
> You redeemed us from the house of bondage ...
> You split apart the waters of the Red Sea,
> The faithful you rescued, the wicked drowned ...
> Then Your beloved sang hymns of thanksgiving ...
> They acclaimed the King, God on high,
> Great and awesome source of all blessings,
> The ever-living God, exalted in his majesty.
> He humbles the proud and raises the lowly;
> He helps the needy and answers His people's call ...
> Then Moses and all the children of Israel
> Sang with great joy this song to the Lord:
> Who is like You O Lord among the mighty?
> Who is like You, so glorious in holiness?
> So wondrous your deeds, so worthy of praise!
> The redeemed sang a new song to You;
> They sang in chorus at the shore of the sea,
> Acclaiming Your sovereignty with thanksgiving:
> The Lord shall reign for ever and ever.
> Rock of Israel, arise to Israel's defense!
> Fulfill Your promise to deliver Judah and Israel.
> Our redeemer is the Holy One of Israel,
> The Lord of hosts is His name.
> Praised are You, O Lord, redeemer of Israel.

(Hadas 1966: 50 – 1)

fundamentally and essentially just – the starting point and foundation of all else. That demonstration is basic to the ethical monotheism that animates Judaism.

"MEASURE FOR MEASURE" ILLUSTRATED BY THE ORDEAL OF THE WIFE ACCUSED OF ADULTERY

Numbers, Chapter 5, contains the law concerning the wife accused of adultery. As sages interpret that law, it is a demonstration of God's justice. Here is the sages' account of God's justice, which is always commensurate, both for reward and punishment. What we note is the sages' identification of the precision of justice, the exact match of action and reaction, each step in the sin, each step in the response. We notice, above all, the immediacy of God's presence in the entire transaction. God is a person and a presence for the pious Israelite, and here is a transaction that shows precisely what that means. The rabbinic sages draw general conclusions from the specifics of the law that Scripture sets forth:

Mishnah-tractate Sotah 1:7

A. By that same measure by which a man metes out [to others], do they mete out to him:

B. She [the wife accused of adultery] primped herself for sin, the Omnipresent made her repulsive.

C. She exposed herself for sin, the Omnipresent exposed her.

D. With the thigh she began to sin, and afterward with the belly, therefore the thigh suffers the curse first, and afterward the belly.

E. But the rest of the body does not escape [punishment].

The course of response of the woman accused of adultery to her drinking of the bitter water that is supposed to produce one result for the guilty, another for the innocent, is described in Scripture in this language:

If no man has lain with you ... be free from this water of bitterness that brings the curse. But if you have gone astray ... then the Lord make

> you an execration ... when the Lord makes your thigh fall away and
> your body swell; may this water ... pass into your bowels and make
> your body swell and your thigh fall away.
>
> (Num. 5:20–2).

This is amplified and expanded, extended to the entire rite, where
the woman is disheveled; then the order, thigh, belly, shows the
perfect precision of the penalty. What Scripture treats as a case,
sages transform into a generalization, so making Scripture yield
governing rules. And the main point, that God governs justly,
derived from those rules based on the facts of Scripture.

THE PROBLEM OF EVIL

Whatever happens, therefore, happens because God wants it to be.
But monotheism by its nature raises the problem of God's justice.
That is because monotheism attributes to one God responsibility
for all that happens and at the same time assigns to him the attributes of justice and mercy. These convictions concerning God's
nature produce conflict and yield what is called "the problem of
evil."

That problem asks how come if God is both powerful and just,
manifest injustice flourishes in the world. People point to the prosperity of the wicked and the suffering of the righteous to challenge
God's justice. The book of Job tells how its hero lived an upright life
yet suffered misfortune. How can God be deemed just when worldly
happenings are difficult to justify? And the quality of mercy is
equally difficult to discern. So how can the one, all-powerful, just,
merciful God permit bad things to happen to good people?

HOW JUDAIC MONOTHEISM SOLVES THE PROBLEM
OF EVIL

Justice does not always prevail. If life leads to the grave and ends
there, then the problem of evil that monotheism creates – If God is
One and all-powerful, how come bad things happen to good people?
– has no solution. The one and only God is either powerful and
unjust, or weak and just.

But the Torah, as Judaism reads it, promises life after death and so solves the problem of evil. Every one who lives not only dies but at the end of time rises from the grave and stands in judgment. Those who are justified, who have lived a life that in the balance merits acceptance and forgiveness, enter the Garden of Eden or the world to come (the language of resurrection and eternal life is diverse). The wicked are judged for extinction and cease to be.

How does God's rule beyond the grave resolve the problem of evil? It provides for another chapter in the story of a person's life, an opportunity to right the wrongs and restore the balance in each person's narrative. True, good things happen to bad people in this world, and so too bad things to good people, but with Resurrection and Judgment the wicked receive their just desserts, and the righteous their reward for goodness. There consequently is no problem of evil, there is only the doctrine of God's justice and mercy for all creatures. This doctrine is expressed in the following way:

Tractate Abot 4:21

A. R. Eliezer Haqqappar says, "Those who are born are destined to die, and those who die are destined for resurrection.

B. "And the living are destined to be judged so as to know, to make known, and to confirm that (1) he is God, (2) he is the one who forms, (3) he is the one who creates, (4) he is the one who understands, (5) he is the one who judges, (6) he is the one who gives evidence, (7) he is the one who brings suit, (8) and he is the one who is going to make the ultimate judgment.

C. "Blessed be he, for before him are not (1) guile, (2) forgetfulness, (3) respect for persons, (4) bribe taking, for everything is his.

D. "And know that everything is subject to reckoning.

E. "And do not let your evil impulse persuade you that Sheol is a place of refuge for you.

F. "For (1) despite your wishes were you formed, (2) despite your wishes were you born, (3) despite your wishes do you live, (4) despite your wishes do you die, (5) despite your wishes are you going to give a

> full accounting before the King of kings of kings,
> the Holy One, blessed be he King of kings of kings,
> the Holy One, blessed be he."

God, thus, rules the lives of all who pass through this world and sees to it that ultimately, at the end of time, justice is done for all. These convictions do not take the form of abstract propositions about the end of days beyond the last horizon. They infuse the emotional life of Israelites who believe that God is a perpetual presence, recording all that happens and remembering it, as we saw in connection with the Days of Awe, the annual accounting.

HOW DOES THE TORAH PROVE THE MERCY OF GOD?

When it comes to the last judgment, we need hardly be reminded that God judges in a merciful manner. If the balance is equal, then God inclines the scale to forgiveness. Mercy complements justice, so that justice is not possible without mercy. That is consistent with the love that God lavishes on his creatures, to which we referred earlier. Now we see how God's mercy tempers justice in judgment:

Yerushalmi-tractate Sanhedrin 10:1 I:2:

H. If the greater part of his record consisted of honorable deeds, and the smaller part, transgressions, they exact punishment from him [in this world].

I. If the smaller part of the transgressions which he has done are of the lesser character, [he is punished] in this world so as to pay him his full and complete reward in the world to come.

J. If the greater part of his record consisted of transgressions and the lesser part of honorable deeds, they pay him off with the reward of the religious deeds which he has done entirely in this world, so as to exact punishment from him in a whole and complete way in the world to come.

K. If the greater part of his record consisted of honorable deeds, he will inherit the Garden of Eden. If

> the greater part consisted of transgressions, he will inherit Gehenna.

Now we reach the critical point at which mercy enters in:

> L. [If the record] was evenly balanced –
> M. Said R. Yosé b. Haninah, "' ... forgives sins ... ,' is not written here, but rather, ' ... forgives [a] sin' (Num. 14:18). That is to say, the Holy One, blessed be he, tears up one bond [recorded] among the transgressions, so that the honorable deeds then will outweigh the others."
> N. Said R. Eleazar, "'And that to thee, O Lord, belongs steadfast love. For thou dost requite a man according to his work' (Ps. 62:13). 'His deed' is not written here, but 'like his deed' – if he has none, you give him one of yours."
> All Israel has a portion in the world to come.

ALL ISRAEL HAS A PORTION OF THE WORLD TO COME

The basic belief in the Resurrection of the Dead contains two elements that are fundamental: (1) that the Resurrection of the Dead will take place, and (2) that it is the Torah that reveals that the dead will rise. The components of the doctrine fit together, in that statement, in a logical order.

1. In a predictable application of the governing principle of measure for measure, those who do not believe in the Resurrection of the Dead will be punished by being denied what they do not accept. Some few others bear the same fate.

2. But to be an Israelite means to rise from the grave, and that applies to all Israelites. That is to say, the given of the condition of Israel is that the entire Holy People will enter the world to come, which is to say, will enjoy the Resurrection of the Dead and eternal life. "Israel," then, is anticipated to be the people of eternity.

Who is condemned to spend eternity in the grave? These
are those that deny the Resurrection of the Dead, or
reject that teaching of the world to come derives from the
Torah, or who deny that the Torah comes from God, or
hedonists. Excluded from the category of resurrection
and the world to come are only those who by their own
sins have denied themselves that benefit. Scripture also
yields the names of three kings who will not be resur-
rected, as well as four commoners, also specified
generations: The generation of the Flood in the time of
Noah, the generation of the dispersion in the matter of the
Tower of Babel, and the men of Sodom in the time of
Abraham, the generation of the wilderness that rejected
the Land and the party of Korah against Moses, and the
Ten Tribes.

The theology of resurrection figures in the catalogue of judicial
penalties for crimes and sins, whether flogging or capital punishment. Denial of eternal life registers as the worst penalty Judaism
can inflict. Death on its own atones for sins and secures a place for
the criminal in the world to come. That is stated explicitly:

Mishnah-tractate Sanhedrin 6:2

A. [When] he [the man sentenced to death] was ten
    cubits from the place of stoning, they say to him,
    "Confess," for it is usual for those about to be put
    to death to confess.

B. For whoever confesses has a share in the world to
    come.

C. For so we find concerning Achan, to whom Joshua
    said "My son, I pray you, give glory to the Lord, the
    God of Israel, and confess to him, [and tell me now
    what you have done: Hide it not from me.] And
    Achan answered Joshua and said, Truly have I
    sinned against the Lord, the God of Israel and thus
    and thus I have done" (Josh. 7:19).

D. And how do we know that his confession achieved
    atonement for him? For it is said, "And Joshua
    said, Why have you troubled us? The Lord will

> trouble you this day" (Josh. 7:25) — *This day* the
> Lord will trouble you, but you will not be troubled
> in the world to come.

The death penalty secures atonement and opens the way to life in the world to come. That conviction bears in its wake the belief that in dying Israelites atone for their sins and are ready for judgment. That explains why, with few exceptions and for stated reasons, all Israelites have a share in the world to come.

Mishnah-tractate Sanhedrin 10:1 [Bavli-tractate Sanhedrin 11:1]

> A. All Israelites have a share in the world to come,
> B. as it is said, "Your people also shall be all right-
> eous, they shall inherit the land forever; the branch
> of my planting, the work of my hands, that I may
> be glorified" (Isa. 60:21).

That single statement serves better than any other to define Israel. Now we forthwith take up exceptions:

> C. And these are the ones who have no portion in the
> world to come:
> D. He who says, the Resurrection of the Dead is a
> teaching that does not derive from the Torah, and
> the Torah does not come from Heaven; and an
> Epicurean.
> E. R. Aqiba says, "Also: He who reads in heretical books,
> F. "and he who whispers over a wound and says, 'I
> will put none of the diseases upon you which I
> have put on the Egyptians, for I am the Lord who
> heals you'" (Exod. 15:26).
> G. Abba Saul says, "Also: He who pronounces the
> divine Name as it is spelled out."

The prophet, in Scripture, also has provided the basic allegation on which all else rests, that is, "Israel will be entirely righteous and inherit the land forever." Denying the stated dogmas removes a person from the status of "Israel," in line with the opening statement, so to be Israel means to rise from the dead, and Israel as a collectivity is defined as those persons in humanity who are destined to eternal life, a supernatural community. So much for the initial statement of the eschatological doctrine in the oral Torah.

HOW DO WE KNOW THAT THE RESURRECTION OF THE DEAD IS BASIC TO JUDAISM?

The importance of the doctrine of the Resurrection of the Dead is shown by its prominent position in the daily prayers of faithful Israelites. Three times a day, a prescribed prayer is recited, and within that prayer is an explicit affirmation of God's promise to keep faith with those that lie in the dust, language that appears in the prayer books of Reform Judaism as much as in those of Orthodox and Conservative Judaism.

> Your might, O Lord, is eternal;
> Your saving power brings the dead to life again.
> You sustain the living with loving kindness;
> With great mercy you bring the dead to life again.
> You support the fallen, heal the sick, free the captives.
> You keep faith with those who sleep in the dust.
> Who can compare with your might, O lord and King?
> You are master over life and death and deliverance.
> Faithful are you in bringing the dead to life again.
> Praised are you, O Lord, master over life and death.
>
> (Hadas 1966: 55–6)

So we see the worldview of Judaism as a coherent and systematic statement of ethical monotheism, with the Israelite called upon to take up citizenship in the Kingdom of God and promised eternal life as the reward. To be an Israelite is to live forever.

PART III

THE SECULAR HISTORY OF JUDAISM

8

THE FORMATION OF NORMATIVE JUDAISM

Basic Judaism as defined by Scripture took shape in the century following the destruction of the temple of Jerusalem by the Babylonians in 586 B.C.E. At that time, scriptures and traditions of the period from remote antiquity to 586 were gathered together to form the Torah, meaning the Pentateuch, to which were added the prophets and the writings. The Torah told the story of exile and return, possession of the Land, loss of the Land, recovery of the Land. The Torah was interpreted in various ways by different communities of Judaism. Among these were scribes, a profession, and sects such as the Pharisees, Sadducees, Essenes, the community that produced the Dead Sea library, and the Jesus movement. After the Romans destroyed the temple in 70 C.E., the Christians went their own way. The Pharisees and scribes carried forward the oral traditions that were associated with the Torah and formed the community of Judaism that observed the written Torah in accord with these oral traditions. That community called its authorities "rabbis," hence is known as rabbinic. Its principal book after Scripture was the Talmud, so it is known as Talmudic Judaism. Its possession of written and oral traditions earned for it the title, "the Judaism of the dual Torah," written and oral. Over the millennium from 70 to about 1000 C.E., Rabbinic Judaism became normative.

FROM STORY TO HISTORY

Having surveyed the basic story told *by* normative Judaism, we now take up the basic history *of* that Judaism. The one comes from a participant, the other, an observer from the outside. Chapters 2 through 7 tell the story as it is told by participants in normative Judaism. Here and in the following chapters, we review the story as it is told by outsiders, specifically by historians of religion.

The participant in a religious tradition tells its story, seeing the episodes to form a whole in the coherent narrative. The observer of that same system, standing outside, studies the history of the story, examining the parts in their several distinct political contexts: Who told the story, with what variations, under what circumstances, and, above all, when and in answer to what questions? The believer defines as unique and true the story that is told. The outsider collects a variety of stories and compares and contrasts them. So we move from story to history.

The main point is simple. The insiders tell a single set of stories. But for a long time, there were competing narratives, different stories told by different communities of Judaism. Only after many centuries did the basic set of stories told in Chapters 2 through 7 attain the status of the norm. Then emerged the official and orthodox definition of the way of life, worldview, and social entity ("Israel") which we deem basic.

The competing stories flourished for a long time, from *c*. 450 B.C.E. to *c*. 70 C.E., and for that reason, we distinguish between the story told *by* Judaism and the history *of* Judaism. The story as we have surveyed it represents a particular choice among Scripture's narratives and a purposeful arrangement and shaping of those stories that were selected.

What is the difference between story told *by*, and history *of*, Judaism? The story told by Judaism as we surveyed it in Chapters 2 through 7 takes up Creation and Exodus, Torah and Sinai, exile and return. The history of that Judaism, for its part, asks what actually happened and how we know.

Now, accordingly, we shift our perspective from that of the participants in the tradition – the ones that tell the story about themselves – to that of the observer of the tradition, tracing its actual history.

THE PENTATEUCH IN HISTORICAL CONTEXT

It was only after the destruction of the First Temple of Jerusalem in 586 B.C.E. that the Torah, that is, the five books of Moses, came into being, a pastiche of received stories, some old, some new, all revised for the purposes of the final compilers and editors. What precipitated the compilation of stories into a continuous narrative, the Torah? It was the loss of the temple in 586 B.C.E. and the restoration of Israel to the Land of Israel a half century later. The Persian conquerors of Babylonia then gave the Israelite exiles permission to return to the Land of Israel and to rebuild the temple. In the aftermath of the destruction and the later restoration of the exiles to the Land, the priests and Ezra the Scribe wrote out in Scripture the answer to the fundamental question of Israelite existence: How to hold on to the Land this time?

Israel's history formed the story of how, despite the prophets' persistent warnings and because of its conduct, Israel lost its land, first in the north, then in the south. From the exile in Babylonia and return to Zion some decades later, a single conclusion was to be drawn. That was, nothing was a given, everything was a gift based on conditions. The authorship of the Torah recast Israel's history into the story of the conditional existence of the people. The Pentateuchal narrative drew the consequences of the Israelites' experience of possessing, losing, and being restored to the Land. They knew things that Israel before 586 B.C.E. could never have imagined: The experience of exile and return.

The Pentateuch then was completed by Ezra the Scribe in about 450 B.C.E. It set forth a collective story of exile and return, of a peoplehood subject to condition and stipulation, forever threatened with desolation, always requiring renewal. To Israel, the Torah imparted the picture of society subject to judgment, and the story of exile and return and the conditional possession of the Land embodied that picture.

SECOND TEMPLE JUDAISMS, 450 B.C.E. TO 70 C.E.

The temple priests and Torah scribes who sponsored the Pentateuch were not the only group that offered its explanation of what had happened and its meaning. Three types of Judaic systems – ways of life, worldviews, theories of what and who is Israel – emerged to compete from 450 B.C.E. to 70 C.E., when the Second Temple was destroyed. The systems centered upon three types or points of emphasis:

1. The priests stressed doctrine, law, way of life, emerging from the priestly viewpoint, with its interest in sanctification.
2. The visionaries – seekers after the meaning and end of events – emphasized the meaning and end of history, produced by the prophetic angle of vision, with a focus on salvation.
3. The sages seeking wisdom took a special interest in the wise conduct of everyday affairs, yielded by the wisdom writings, with a stress on the here and now of ordinary life.

Ancient Israel's heritage yielded (1) the sacrificial cult with its priests, and (2) the prophetic and apocalyptic hope for meaning in history and the end of days embodied in Messiahs and (3) the Torah, with its scribes and teachers. The priestly vision predominated in the Pentateuch, the historical vision in the prophetic writings, and the wisdom vision in Job, Qoheleth (Ecclesiastes), Proverbs, Psalms, and other wisdom writings.

So ancient Israel produced three ideal types: priest, messianic soldier seeking the end of days, and sage. Viewed as ideal types, the Judaic systems in Second Temple times yielded three ways of life:

1. The priest described society as organized through lines of structure flowing outward from the temple. The priestly caste stood at the top of a social scale in which all things were properly organized, each with its correct name and proper place. The inherent sanctity of Israel, the people, came through genealogy to its fullest embodiment in the priest. Food set aside for his rations at God's command

possessed that same sanctity; so too did the table at which he ate his food. To the priest, the sacred society of Israel produced history as an account of what happened in, and on occasion to, the temple.

2. As for prophecy's insistence that the fate of the nation depended upon the faith and moral condition of society, history testified to the external context and inner condition of Israel, viewed as a whole. Both sage and priest saw Israel from the aspect of eternity. But the nation lived out its life in the history of this world, among other peoples coveting the very same Land, within the politics of empires. The Messiah's kingship would resolve the issues of Israel's subordinated relationship to other nations and empires, establishing once for all time the correct context for priest and sage alike.

3. To the sage, the life of society demanded wise regulation. Relationships among people required guidance by the laws embodied in the Torah and best interpreted by the sage. Accordingly, the task of Israel was to construct a way of life in accordance with the revealed rules of the Torah. The sage, master of the rules, stood at the head.

THE SOCIAL WORLD OF SECOND TEMPLE JUDAISM

Among a number of Judaic groups that distinguished themselves between 450 B.C.E. and 70 C.E., we focus on two: first, the Judaic system, by some deemed comparable to that of the Essenes, put forth by the writings found at the Dead Sea site called Qumran, and, second, the Pharisees. Each in its way realized in sharp and extreme form the ideals of the normative system of the priests' and scribes' Torah of Moses.

Both the community represented by the library found at Qumran and the Pharisees stressed cultic cleanness and uncleanness. In Leviticus and Numbers, people are supposed to preserve temple and priestly food and utensils from uncleanness, such as is described in Leviticus 11–15 and Numbers 19 – corpse-contamination, for example. Priests were supposed to keep those laws when they made offerings to God at the altar and when they ate their share of the offerings assigned to them as rations. The Pharisees and the community represented by the library at Qumran extended that concern to lay people eating their ordinary food at home. They were lay people pretending to be priests.

Thus, the Judaism represented by the writings found at Qumran observed a set of rules of cultic cleanness when eating their meals at home. So, too, the Pharisees were (among other points of definition) people bound by shared observance of common rules governing the preparation and eating of meals. This was to be done in accord with the regulations of purity that applied to the priesthood in consuming the food they received in the temple. Both groups imitated the priests and so entered into that state of holiness achieved by the priests in the temple. Each of these social groups defined itself around the eating of cultic meals in the state of cleanness prescribed by Leviticus for temple priests in the eating of their share of the temple sacrifices.

QUMRAN'S JUDAIC SYSTEM

The Judaic religious system portrayed by the library found at the Dead Sea flourished in the last two centuries B.C.E. down to 68 C.E. The main component of the worldview of the library's Judaism was the conviction that the community formed the saving remnant of Israel, and that God would shortly annihilate the wicked. These members of the true Israel would be saved, because their founder, the teacher of righteousness, established a new contract or covenant between the community and God. So this Israel would endure. The task of the community was to remain faithful to the covenant, to endure the exile in the wilderness, and to prepare for the restoration of the temple in its correct form. So the community recapitulated the history of Israel, seeing itself as the surviving remnant of some disaster that has destroyed the faith, preparing for that restoration that they anticipated would soon come – just as it had before.

In all, therefore, we find in the Qumran system a replication of the Judaic system of the priesthood, with one important qualification. While the Judaic system represented by the Pentateuch laid great stress on the enduring and holy way of life, the Qumran system as represented by its library added a powerful element of conviction that the end of days was at hand and so combined the holy way of life with a doctrine of salvation at the end of time. The principal components of the scriptural composite – Torah laws, prophetic historical interpretation, sagacious rules on the conduct of everyday life – found counterparts in the library of the Qumran community. The Qumran Judaism reworked the several strands into a distinctive and characteristic statement of its own.

The Qumran library sets forth the Judaic system of a holy community in the here and now, awaiting the climax of the end of days. The elements of the original system are three: First, the notion of a saving remnant, a chosen few, which surely originated in the pattern of Israel that endured beyond 586 B.C.E.; second, the conception of a community with a historical beginning, middle, and end, rather than a community that exists more or less permanently; third, the notion that the Israel at hand realizes in its being the sanctification of the temple. All commentators on the library of Qumran have found striking the community's sense of itself as different, separate from the rest of Israel, the clean few among the unclean many, the saved few, the children of light as against the children of darkness. The fundamental notion that the small group constituted in microcosm the Israel that mattered rests on the premise that the Israel out there, the nation as a whole, lives on condition and responds to stipulation.

Making distinctions within the old Israel in favor of the new to begin with requires the conviction that the life of Israel is a status to be achieved, a standing to be attained through appropriate sanctification. And that basic notion in detail expresses the general pattern of the Pentateuchal structure: Israel is called, formed as something out of nothing, a very particular entity, subject to very special conditions: The children of light, as against the rest, the children of darkness.

THE SCRIBES AND THE PHARISEES BEFORE 70 C.E.

Two groups that flourished in Second Temple times, the scribes and the Pharisees – one a profession, the other a sect – made an important contribution to the formation of Rabbinic Judaism after 70 C.E. The scribes carried forward the traditions of interpreting the Torah. The Pharisees emphasized the holiness of all Israelites and contributed the stress on preserving the sanctity of Israel. These matters of Torah learning and living the holy way of life formed principal components of Rabbinic Judaism.

The scribes were sages of the law of the Torah, teaching the interpretation of the Torah and drawing up valid documents for the administration of the law. The Pharisees, another Israelite community of lay people pretending to be priests and eating their food in accord with the priestly regulations, are important in the history of Judaism because they formed a principal part of Rabbinic Judaism after 70 C.E.

The message of the one – the matter of sanctification contributed by the Pharisees – joined with the method – the wisdom and learning of the scribes – of the other. The first document of Rabbinic Judaism, the Mishnah, c. 200 C.E., joined the scribes' method and the priests' and Pharisees' doctrines.

The Pharisees stressed observing in everyday, secular circumstances the temple rules of sanctification, including tithing. Laws governing what may be eaten and under what circumstances were dietary laws. Keeping of the laws concerning the correct preparation of food, including the proper separation, for the support of the priesthood and other scheduled castes, of a portion of the crops formed one of the requirements of membership in the Pharisaic sect. Scripture had specified a variety of rules on the matter, in general holding that God owned a share of the crops, and God's share was to go to the holy castes (Priests, Levites). When Pharisees made sure that everything that was supposed to yield its portion to the scheduled castes did, they therefore obeyed those rules concerning the preparation of food that linked meals to the altar and its service.

The book of Leviticus had furthermore laid down rules governing uncleanness, its sources and effects. The result of contact with such sources of uncleanness was not hygienic but, mainly, cultic: One affected by uncleanness could not enter the temple (Lev. 12, 13–14). Another result of uncleanness deriving from certain sources was to prohibit sexual relations (Lev. 15), but one made unclean in that way also could not go to the temple. The concern for the cleanness or uncleanness of utensils and persons, therefore, for the authors of Leviticus and Numbers derived from the protection of the cult and the temple from those dangers seen to lurk in the sources of uncleanness, which was death or things comparable to death.

What was at stake in the stress on preserving cultic cleanness? The Pharisees, by all accounts, affirmed the eternity of the soul (as Josephus, the Jewish historian of Judaism of the late first century C.E., says) and the resurrection of the dead (as the New Testament Luke's picture of Paul in Acts maintains). Sanctification led beyond the uncleanness of the grave to purification out of the most unclean of all sources of uncleanness, the realm of death itself. The dead would rise up for salvation at the end of days. So the two basic components of Rabbinic Judaism, Torah study and practice, and sanctification in the here and now and salvation at the end of days, derived from pre-70 C.E. scribism and Pharisaism.

THE FIRST PHASE OF RABBINIC JUDAISM, 70–200 C.E.: THE JUDAISM OF THE MISHNAH

Portrayed by the Mishnah, *c.* 200 C.E., the first phase of Rabbinic Judaism was continuous with pre-70 C.E. Pharisaism and scribism with their emphases on sanctification and wisdom, respectively. Rabbinic Judaism responded to the destruction of the Temple in 70 C.E. by maintaining that the holiness of the life of Israel, the people, a holiness that had formerly centered on the temple, still endured. Israel's sanctification, thus, transcended the physical destruction of the building and the cessation of sacrifices. Israel the people was holy, was the medium and the instrument of God's sanctification.

Sanctity persists, indelibly, in Israel, the people, in its way of life, in its land, in its priesthood, in its food, in its mode of sustaining life, in its manner of procreating and so sustaining the nation. That judgment is expressed in the Halakhah, the law, set forth in the flagship tractate of the Mishnah, tractate Hullin (on food preparation for everyday meals, not those for the priests in the temple). The same principle recurs at Mishnah Hullin 5:1, 6:1, 7:1, 10:1, 11:1, and 12:1. The Mishnah's legislation recognizes that the destruction of the temple in 70 C.E., as in 586 B.C.E., marked a change in Israel's holy life. But the sanctity of Israel endures beyond the loss of the holy city, the holy temple, and, ultimately, the holy land. The events of 132–5 C.E. registered in the same context. We examine a single rule concerning dietary laws to see how the Mishnah formulates that view. The same pattern is repeated throughout.

Mishnah Hullin 5:1

[The prohibition against slaughtering on the same day] it and its young (Lev. 22:28) applies (1) in the Land and outside the Land, (2) in the time of the Temple and not in the time of the Temple, (3) in the case of unconsecrated beasts and in the case of consecrated beasts.

The tripartite formulation, (1) "Time of the Temple / not in the time of the Temple" or (2) "in the Land and outside the Land" or (3) in the case of what is unconsecrated as much as in the case of what is consecrated, explicitly recognizes that the destruction of the temple marked a boundary in the situation of Israel. The limits of the Land marked another. The status as to sanctification recorded a third. The question then was, do these marks of sanctification – temple, land, consecration – apply now that the temple and priest-hood have ceased to function? The specified rites pertain in the present age, when the temple lies in ruins, and in the present situa-tion, when Israel is located outside of the Holy Land. Israel the Holy People remains holy and subject to the disciplines of sanctifi-cation, the priesthood remains holy and worthy of receiving its rations, which form part of the disciplines of sanctification of the produce and the yield of the Land.

The Mishnah's system therefore focused upon the holiness of the life of Israel, the people, a holiness that had formerly centered on the temple. The system then instructed Israel to act as if there was a new temple formed of Israel, the Holy People. Joined to the Pharisaic mode of looking at life, now centered in the doctrine of the holiness of Israel the people, was the substance of the scribal ideal, the stress on learning of Torah and carrying out its teachings. The emerging system would claim, like the scribes of old, that it was possible to serve God not only through sacrifice, but also through study of Torah. So the question is the question of the priests and Pharisees: How to serve God? But the answer is the answer of the scribes: Through Torah learning. For the relationship between Scripture and the Mishnah in a particular case, see Box 8.1.

The Pharisaic method, with its stress on the everyday sanctifica-tion of all Israel joined with the scribal message, with its stress on

BOX 8.1 MISHNAH AND SCRIPTURE

The question of how the Mishnah and Scripture treat the same problem emerges when we compare the same case as it emerges in both documents. The issue is how to resolve conflicting claims to the same object. Here is Scripture's version of the problem.

> Then two harlots came to the King and stood before him. The one woman said, "Oh, my lord, this woman and I dwell in the same house; and I gave birth to a child while she was in the house. Then on the third day after I was delivered, this woman also gave birth, and we were alone; there was no one else with us in the house. Only we two were in the house. And this woman's son died in the night, because she lay on it. And she arose at midnight and took my son from beside me, while your maidservant slept, and laid it in my bosom. When I rose in the morning to nurse my child, behold, it was dead; but when I looked at it closely in the morning, behold, it was not the child that I had borne."
>
> But the other woman said, "No, the living child is mine, and the dead child is yours."
>
> The first said, "No, the dead child is yours, and the living child is mine."
>
> Thus they spoke before the King.
>
> Then the King said, "The one says, 'This is my son that is alive, and your son is dead,' and the other says, 'No, but your son is dead, and my son is the living one'."
>
> And the King said, "Bring me a sword."
>
> So a sword was brought before the King. And the King said, "Divide the living child in two and give half to the one and half to the other."
>
> Then the woman whose son was alive said to the King, because her heart yearned for her son, "Oh, my lord, give her the living child and by no means slay it."
>
> But the other said, "It shall be neither mine nor yours; divide it."
>
> Then the King answered and said, "Give the living child to the first woman and by no means slay it; she is its mother."
>
> And all Israel heard of the judgment that the King had rendered,

and they stood in awe of the King, because they perceived that the wisdom of God was in him, to render justice.

(1 Kgs. 3:16 – 28)

Here is the Mishnah's version of the same problem.

Mishnah-tractate Baba Mesia 1:1 – 2

1:1

Two lay hold of a cloak –
this one says, "I found it!" –
and that one says, "I found it!" –
this one says, "It's all mine!" –
and that one says, "It's all mine!" –
this one takes an oath that he possesses no less a share of it than half,
and that one takes an oath that he possesses no less a share of it than half,
and they divide it up.
This one says, "It's all mine!" –
and that one says, "Half of it is mine!"
the one who says, "It's all mine!" takes an oath that he possesses no less of a share of it than three parts,
and the one who says, "Half of it is mine!" takes an oath that he possesses no less a share of it than a fourth part.
This one then takes three shares, and that one takes the fourth.

1:2

Two were riding on a beast,
or one was riding and one was leading it –
this one says, "It's all mine!" –
and that one says, "It's all mine!" –
this one takes an oath that he possesses no less a share of it than half,
and that one takes an oath that he possesses no less a share of it than half.
And they divide it.

But when they concede [that they found it together] or have witnesses to prove it, they divide [the beast's value] without taking an oath.

It is difficult to imagine two more different ways of saying more or less the same thing. The Mishnah's author speaks in brief clauses; he uses no adjectives; he requires mainly verbs. He has no actors, no "they did thus and so." He speaks only of actions people take in the established situation. No one says anything, as against, "the King said … " There is only the rule, no decision to be made for the case in particular. There is no response to the rule, no appeal to feeling.

Indeed, the Mishnah's author knows nothing of emotions. Scripture tells us, "because her heart yearned," and the Mishnah's author knows nothing of the particularity of cases, while to the Scripture's narrator, that is the center of matters. The Mishnah presents rules; Scripture exceptions. The Mishnah speaks of the social order; Scripture, special cases. The Mishnah addresses all Israel, and its principal player – the community at large – is never identified; Scripture tells us about the individual, embodied in the divinely chosen monarch, and relates the story of Israel through the details of his reign.

the Torah. As we saw just now, Pharisaism laid stress upon universal keeping of the law, obligating every Jew to do what only the elite – the priests – were normally expected to accomplish. The professional ideal of the scribes stressed the study of the Torah and the centrality of the learned person in the religious system. But there was something more. It was the doctrine of Israel and that made all the difference. If the worldview came from the scribes, the way of life from the Pharisees, the doctrine of who is Israel – and the social reality beyond the doctrine – was fresh and unpredictable. It was surviving Israel, beyond the caesura marked by the destruction of the temple.

The stress of the initial statement of Rabbinic Judaism – the Mishnah's – accordingly lies on sanctification, understood as the correct arrangement of all things, each in its proper category, each called by its rightful name. This was just as at the creation, everything having been given its proper name, God called the natural world very good and sanctified it.

The world addressed by the Mishnah, however, is hardly congruent to the worldview of a well-ordered society presented within the Mishnah. In the aftermath of the war against Rome in 132– 5 C.E., the temple was declared permanently prohibited to Jews, and Jerusalem was closed off to them as well. So there was no cult, no temple, no Holy City, to which, at this time, the description of the Mishnaic laws applied. A sizable proportion of the Mishnah deals with matters to which the rabbinic sages had no material access or practical knowledge at the time of their work.

For the Mishnah contains among its six divisions a division on the conduct of the cult, namely, the fifth, as well as one on the conduct of matters so as to preserve the cultic purity of the sacrificial system along the lines laid out in Leviticus, the sixth division. In fact, a fair part of the second division, on appointed times, takes up the conduct of the cult on special days, for example, the sacrifices offered on the Day of Atonement, Passover, and the like. Indeed, what the Mishnah wants to know about appointed seasons concerns the cult far more than it does the synagogue. The fourth division, on civil law, for its part, presents an elaborate account of a political structure and system of Israelite self-government, in tractates Sanhedrin and Makkot, not to mention Shebuot and Horayot. This system speaks of king, priest, temple, and court. But it was not the Jews, their kings, priests, and judges, but the Romans, who conducted the government of Israel in the Land of Israel in the time in which the second-century authorities did their work. So it would appear that well over half of the document before us speaks of cult, temple, government, priesthood.

When we consider that, in the very time in which the authorities before us did their work, the temple lay in ruins, the city of Jerusalem was prohibited to Israelites, and the Jewish government and administration that had centered on the temple and based its authority on the holy life lived there were in ruins, the fantastic character of the Mishnah's address to its own catastrophic day becomes clear. Much of the Mishnah speaks of matters not in being in the time in which the Mishnah was created. That is because the Mishnah wishes to make its statement on what really matters.

In the age beyond catastrophe, the problem was to reorder a world off course and adrift, to gain reorientation for an age in which the sun has come out after the night and the fog. The Mishnah is a document of imagination and fantasy, describing how things ought to be, as reconstructed out of the shards and remnants of reality, but, in larger measure, building social being out of beams of hope. The Mishnah tells us something about how things were, but everything about how a small group of rabbinic sages wanted things to be. The document is orderly, repetitious, careful in both language and message. It is small-minded, picayune, obvious, dull, routine – everything its age was not.

The Mishnah's principal message is that man is at the center of creation, the head of all creatures upon Earth, corresponding to God in Heaven, in whose image man is made. The way in which the Mishnah makes this simple and fundamental statement is to impute power to man to inaugurate and initiate those corresponding processes, sanctification and uncleanness, that play so critical a role in the Mishnah's account of reality. The will of man, expressed through the deed of man, is the active power in the world.

So, stated briefly, the question taken up by the Mishnah and answered by Judaism is, "What can a man do?" And the answer laid down by the Mishnah is, "Man, through will and deed, is master of this world, the measure of all things." Since when the Mishnah thinks of man, it means the Israelite, who is the subject and actor of its system, the statement is clear. This man is Israel, who can do what he wills. In the aftermath of the two wars, the message of the Mishnah cannot have proved more pertinent – or poignant and tragic.

The first of the two stages of the formation of Rabbinic Judaism, therefore, answered a single encompassing question: "What, in the aftermath of the destruction of the holy place and holy cult, remained of the sanctity of the holy caste, the priesthood, of the holy Land, and, above all, of the holy people and its holy way of life?" The answer would endure: Sanctity persists indelibly in Israel, the people, in its way of life, in its Land, in its priesthood, in its food, in its mode of sustaining life, in its manner of procreating and so sustaining the nation. But that answer found itself absorbed, in time to come, within a successor system with its own points of stress and emphasis. For another event, as decisive as the destruction of the Second Temple in 70 C.E., would precipitate another crisis of faith and fate.

THE SECOND PHASE OF RABBINIC JUDAISM, 200–600 C.E.: THE JUDAISM OF THE TALMUDS

Pagan Rome, which had persecuted Christianity for 300 years, in 312 declared Christianity licit and in the next century made it the state religion. Judaism for those same 300 years had pretended to ignore Christianity, despite its claim to form the continuation of Israel. Now, in documents that came to closure in the fourth and fifth centuries C.E., Rabbinic Judaism responded and adapted itself to a new program of issues. Christianity defined those issues: The claim of Christianity to interpret the true meaning of the Hebrew Scriptures as the Old Testament, of prophecy as the prediction of the coming of Jesus Christ, now found validation in events.

What happened with the legalization of Christianity followed by its establishment as the official religion of the Roman Empire was a world-historical change, one that could not be absorbed into Israel's available system of theories on the outsiders, in general, and the meaning of the history of the great empires, in particular. We have already noted the rabbinic patterning of history in the four great empires – Babylonia, Media, Greece, and Rome – to be followed by the fifth and final world empire, Israel, in the end of history itself. Now pagan Rome gave way to Christian Rome, and Rabbinic Judaism had to adapt to the new world.

The Christian empire was fundamentally different from its pagan predecessor in two ways.

First, it shared with Israel reverence for exactly the same holy scriptures on which Jewry based its existence. So it was no longer a wholly other, entirely alien empire that ruled over the horizon. It was now a monotheist, formerly persecuted, biblical empire, not awfully different from Israel in its basic convictions about important matters of time and eternity. And it was near at hand and interested.

Second, established policies of more than half a millennium, from the time of the Maccabees' alliance with Rome to the start of the fourth century, now gave way. Tolerance by the Roman Empire of Judaism and an accommodation with the Jews in their land – disrupted only by the Jews' own violation of the terms of the agreement in 70 and 132 C.E. – now no longer governed. Instead, we find intolerance of Judaism and persecution of Jews through attacks on their persons and property.

The sages worked out their response in the pages of the Talmud of the Land of Israel of *c.* 400 C.E. and in the scriptural commentaries of the age, particularly Genesis Rabbah, *c.* 400 C.E., a commentary to the book of Genesis, and Leviticus Rabbah, *c.* 450 C.E., a commentary to the book of Leviticus. There we identify answers to the urgent questions posed by political change. Specifically, the rabbis put forth a system for salvation. They found in the Mishnah a clear statement that sanctification, including cleanness for the cult and for meals, leads to salvation:

Mishnah-tractate Sotah 9:15

R. Pinhas b. Yair says, "Heedfulness leads to cleanliness, cleanliness leads to cleanness, cleanness leads to abstinence, abstinence leads to holiness, holiness leads to modesty, modesty leads to the fear of sin, the fear of sin leads to piety, piety leads to the Holy Spirit, the Holy Spirit leads to the Resurrection of the Dead, and the Resurrection of the Dead comes through Elijah, blessed be his memory, Amen."

Now sanctification and holiness form way stations on the path to salvation, Resurrection of the Dead and the advent of Elijah, prefiguring the Messiah, that is, the end of days. So Rabbinic Judaism responded to the political changes of the age. They took account of implications for the meaning and end of history as Israel would experience it. This they did when they laid fresh emphasis on salvation. That entailed the introduction of the figure of the Messiah as a principal figure in the purpose of history and its goal. That required the statement of a theory of last things, articulating the conception of Last Judgment and restoration of the dead to life eternal for the system as a whole. All of these initiatives answered the questions involved in the legalization of Christianity as state religion.

The questions were raised by triumphant Christian theologians; the answers provided by the Judaic sages. The former held that the

Christian triumph confirmed the Christhood of Jesus, the rejection of Israel, the end of Israel's hope for salvation at the end of time. The latter offered the Torah in its dual media, the affirmation of Israel as children of Abraham, Isaac, and Jacob, the coming of the Messiah at the end of time. The questions and answers fit the challenge of the age.

At those very specific points at which the Christian challenge met Israel's worldview head on, sages' doctrines responded. What did Israel's sages have to present as the Torah's answer to the Christian challenge? First, there was the Bible, the Old and the New Testaments together. To that challenge the response was the Torah. This response took three forms. The Torah was defined in the doctrine, first, of the status, as oral and memorized revelation, of the Mishnah, and, by implication, of other rabbinical writings. The Torah, moreover, was presented as the encompassing symbol of Israel's salvation. The Torah, finally, was embodied in the person of the Messiah who, of course, would be a rabbi. The Torah in all three modes confronted the cross, with its doctrine of the triumphant Christ, Messiah and king, ruler now of Earth as of Heaven.

The outcome was stunning success for that society for which, to begin with, sages, and, in sages' view, God, cared so deeply: Eternal Israel after the flesh. For Judaism, in the rabbis' statement, did endure in the Christian West, imparting to Israel the secure conviction of constituting that Israel after the flesh to which the Torah continued to speak.

We know sages' Judaism won because when, in turn, Islam gained its victory, Christianity throughout the Middle East and North Africa gave way, leaving only pockets of the faithful to live out the long story of Islamic dominance. But sages' Judaism in those same vast territories retained the loyalty and conviction of the people of the Torah. The cross would rule only where the crescent and its sword did not. But the Torah of Sinai everywhere and always governed in its chosen venue, the community of Judaism calling itself Israel. That was sanctified Israel in time and promised secure salvation for eternity. Why did Rabbinic Judaism succeed within the community of Israel, and what explains its status as normative? To that question we now turn.

9

THE ARTICULATION OF NORMATIVE JUDAISM

Rabbinic Judaism became normative over the first ten centuries C.E. The fourth-century challenge of the rise of monotheist Christianity was followed by the seventh-century challenge of the advent of monotheist Islam. Just as the vast majority of Jews stood firm when Christianity pointed to its political success as evidence of its truth, so they affirmed their loyalty to Judaism when Islam called. By contrast, in the Middle East and North Africa Christianity lost vast, ancient populations to the appeal of Islam.

The Judaic religious system that took shape in the first six centuries C.E. came to predominate. We know that that is the fact because that Judaic system showed resilience in the face of challenges of new modes of thought. Philosophy entered into Rabbinic Judaism and its modes of thought were accepted. Mysticism also entered into Rabbinic Judaism and its doctrines were taken over. These two important facts show the strength of Rabbinic Judaism to deal with change.

Not only so, but that same Rabbinic system defined the character of heresy. Its orthodoxy, first, encompassed the belief in the dual Torah, written as interpreted by the oral. A dissenting ("heretic") system, Karaism, rejected the doctrine of an oral Torah and fixed solely on the written Torah. In these two ways – capacity to accommodate new modes of thought, power to define the agenda of dissent – Rabbinic Judaism showed its normative standing.

THE SUCCESS OF RABBINIC JUDAISM IN WESTERN CIVILIZATION

Rabbinic Judaism predominated from late antiquity to our own day and shapes most contemporary Judaisms, as we shall see in Chapter 10. Its success derives not only from its power to turn the Scripture into the tale of exile and return. Rabbinic Judaism succeeded because that Judaism remained relevant to the urgent questions Jews faced and provided them with, to them self-evidently valid, answers. The Jewish people, through the ages, wanted Judaism to endure and accepted severe disabilities and even persecution, exile, and martyrdom, to sustain that religious tradition. When, in the nineteenth century, Jews thought that their place in politics had shifted, they raised new questions and formed new Judaic systems to answer those questions, as we shall see in the next chapter.

Rabbinic Judaism met head on the challenge of Christianity, and later on of Islam: How can Israel be God's first love yet subordinated to Christian or Muslim rule? This it did by explaining the condition of Israel, the Holy People, in the world governed by other monotheisms than the Israelite one. But Judaism endured in the Christian West as well as in the Muslim East, for a second reason. Christianity and Islam permitted it. The fate of paganism in the fourth and fifth centuries under triumphant Christianity and of Iranian Zoroastrianism and "Sabaeism" in the seventh and eighth centuries under early Islam shows the importance of that factor. It was not the intellectual power of sages alone that secured the long-term triumph of Judaism.

It also was, first, the Christian emperors' policy toward Judaism. This afforded toleration. The religious worship of practitioners of Judaism never was prohibited. Pagan sacrifice, by contrast, came under interdict in 341 C.E. Festivals of theirs went on into the fifth century, but the die was cast. The same could have been the fate of Judaism in Christian Europe. When, in the reconquest of Spain, the Catholic monarchs wanted to wipe Judaism out of Spain, in 1492 they did so. Christian toleration in Poland and other areas of eastern Europe allowed Judaism to continue.

Islam, second, tolerated the Jewish minority and permitted the practice of Judaism. It accorded Jews and Christians subordinated but tolerated standing. Only free male Muslims enjoyed the rank of a full member of society. Jews and Christians could accept Islam or pay a tribute and accept Muslim supremacy, then continuing to practice their received religions.

Rabbinic Judaism constructed for its Israel a world in which the experience of the loss of political sovereignty and the persistence of the condition of tolerated subordination within Islam and Christendom were turned into advantages. The condition of subordination attested to the importance and centrality of Israel in the human situation, in the world order. Just as Israel was punished, so it would be rehabilitated. That rationale for Israel's situation is made explicit in the following story in a document of the third century C.E.

Sifré to Deuteronomy XLIII.III.7–8

7

A. Rabban Gamaliel, R. Joshua, R. Eleazar b. Azariah, and R. Aqiba were going toward Rome. They heard the sound of the city's traffic from as far away as Puteoli, a hundred and twenty *mil* away. They began to cry, while R. Aqiba laughed.

B. They said to him, "Aqiba, why are we crying while you are laughing?"

C. He said to them, "Why are you crying?"

D. They said to him, "Should we not cry, since gentiles, idolators, sacrifice to their idols and bow down to icons, but dwell securely in prosperity, serenely, while the house of the footstool of our God has been put to the torch and left a lair for beasts of the field?"

E. He said to them, "That is precisely why I was laughing. If this is how he has rewarded those who anger him, all the more so [will he reward] those who do his will."

8

A. Another time they went up to Jerusalem and got to Mount Scopus. They tore their garments.

B. They came to the mountain of the house [of the temple] and saw a fox go forth from the house of the holy of holies. They began to cry, while R. Aqiba laughed.

C. They said to him, "You are always giving surprises. We are crying when you laugh!"

D. He said to them, "But why are you crying?"

E. They said to him, "Should we not cry over the place concerning which it is written, 'And the common person who draws near shall be put to death' (Num. 1:51)? Now lo, a fox comes out of it.

F. "In our connection the following verse of Scripture has been carried out: 'For this our heart is faint, for these things our eyes are dim, for the mountain of Zion which is desolate, the foxes walk upon it' (Lam. 5:17–18)."

G. He said to them, "That is the very reason I have laughed. For lo, it is written, 'And I will take for me faithful witnesses to record, Uriah the priest and Zechariah the son of Jeberechiah' (Isa. 8:2).

H. "And what has Uriah got to do with Zechariah? What is it that Uriah said? 'Zion shall be plowed as a field and Jerusalem shall become heaps and the mountain of the Lord's house as the high places of a forest' (Jer. 26:18).

I. "What is it that Zechariah said? 'Thus says the Lord of hosts, "Old men and women shall yet sit in the broad places of Jerusalem (Zech. 8:4).

J. "Said the Omnipresent, 'Lo, I have these two witnesses. If the words of Uriah have been carried out, then the words of Zechariah will be carried out. If the words of Uriah are nullified, then the words of Zechariah will be nullified.

K. "'Therefore I was happy that the words of Uriah have been carried out, so that in the end the words of Zechariah will come about.'"

L.   In this language they replied to him: "Aqiba, you
      have given us comfort."

So the long-term condition of the conquered people turned out to
afford reassurance and make certain the truths of the system. The
success of Judaism derives from this reciprocal process. On the one
side, Rabbinic Judaism restated for Israel in an acutely contemporary form, in terms relevant to the situation of Christendom and
Islam, that experience of loss and restoration, death and resurrection that the Scripture had set forth. But at the same time, Rabbinic
Judaism taught its Israel the lesson that its subordinated position
itself gave probative evidence of the nation's true standing: The low
would be raised up, the humble placed into authority, the proud
reduced, the world made right.

Rabbinic Judaism did more than react, reassure and encourage. It
acted upon and determined the shape of matters. That Judaism for a
long time defined the politics and policy of the community. It
instructed Israel, the Jewish people, on the rules for the formation
of the appropriate world. It laid forth the design for those attitudes
and actions that would yield an Israel both subordinate and tolerated, on the one side, but also proud and hopeful, on the other.

In its full articulation, Rabbinic Judaism began in the encounter
with a successful Christianity and persisted in the face of a still more
successful Islam. But for Israel the people, that Judaism persevered.
That was because, long after the conditions that originally precipitated
the positions and policies deemed normative, that same Judaism not
only reacted to, but also shaped, Israel's condition in the world.
Making a virtue of a policy of subordination, Rabbinic Judaism
defined the Jews' condition and set the limits to its circumstance.

How do we know that Rabbinic Judaism exercised hegemony in
the history of Judaism from antiquity to modern times? That brings
us to the long-term hegemony of Rabbinic Judaism, from antiquity
to modern times. The power of Rabbinic Judaism is attested by two
facts of the history of Judaism from the seventh to the twenty-first
centuries.

First, that Judaic system absorbed within itself massive innova-
tions in modes of thought and media of piety. Its adaptability
showed its interior power to accommodate change. Among them,
for example, a massive rethinking of the very modes of thought of

Judaism, moving from narrative to philosophical thinking, took shape over a long period of time.

Second, that same system so defined issues that heresies took shape in explicit response to its doctrines. Rabbinic Judaism set the agenda for public debate. Heresies defined themselves by rejecting important components of the received system, such as its doctrine (1) of the dual Torah and (2) of the Messiah as a sage and model of the Torah's law fully observed.

SUBSETS OF RABBINIC JUDAISM: NEW PHILOSOPHICAL THINKING

The rise of Islam from the mid-seventh century C.E. brought important intellectual changes, because of the enlightened character of Islamic culture. Specifically, Islam took over the heritage of Greek philosophy and its critical modes of thought and generalization. Rabbinic Judaism accommodated that new mode of thought and produced a statement of philosophical monotheism to complement the narrative statement of monotheism long in place, as we saw in Chapter 7.

Specifically, Muslim theologians, responding to Greek philosophy translated into Arabic (not uncommonly by bilingual Jews), developed a mode of thought along philosophical lines, rigorous, abstract, and scientific, with special interest in a close reading of Aristotle, founder of the philosophical tradition of criticism. Rabbinic sages in the Islamic world then naturalized philosophy within the framework of the dual Torah. They thought philosophically about religious facts and produced theology; and they engaged with counterparts in Islam and Christianity and produced a common philosophy of religion as well.

The new thinking and the issues it generated represented a challenge to the received tradition of doctrine and thought. To be sure, in ancient times a school of Judaic philosophy in the Greek-speaking Jewish world, represented by the Jewish philosopher, Philo of Alexandria, had read Scripture in the light of philosophical modes of thought. But the sages of the Talmud did not follow that generalizing and speculative mode of thought. They read Scripture within a different framework altogether. But as the Judaic intellectuals of Islam faced the challenge of Muslim rationalism and philosophical rigor, they read Scripture and the oral Torah as well in a new way. The task at hand was to reconcile and accommodate the principles of the one with the propositions of the other. In medieval Islam and Christendom, no Judaic intellectuals could rest easy in the admission that Scripture and science, in its philosophical form, came into conflict.

That is why alongside study of Torah – meaning spending one's life in learning the Babylonian Talmud and later codes, commentaries, and rabbinic court decisions – a different sort of intellectual religious life flourished in Judaism. It was the study of the tradition through the instruments of reason and the discipline of philosophy. The philosophical enterprise attracted small numbers of elitists and mainly served their specialized spiritual and intellectual needs. But they set the standard, and those who followed it included the thoughtful and the perplexed – those who took the statements of the tradition most seriously and, through questioning and reflection, intended to examine and then effect them.

The rabbinic philosophers of Judaism, moreover, did not limit their activities to study and teaching. They frequently both occupied high posts within the Jewish community and served in the society of politics, culture, and science outside the community as well. Though not numerous, the philosophers exercised considerable influence, particularly over the mind of an age that believed reason and learning were what really mattered.

The issues of philosophy were set, not by lack of belief, but by deep faith. Few philosophers denied providence, a personal God, and a holy book revealed by God through his chosen messenger. Everyone believed in reward and punishment, in a last judgment, and in a settling of accounts. The Jewish philosopher had to cope with problems imposed not only by the classical faith, but also by the anomalous situation of the Jews themselves. That situation was perceived within the theology of the Torah that told the story of Israel as Adam's counterpart and opposite, covenanted with God. The question of justice loomed large: How was philosophy to account reasonably for a homelessness of God's people, who were well aware that they lived as a minority among powerful, prosperous majorities – Christian or Muslim?

The new context of intellectual competition contributed a new question: If the Torah was true, why did different revelations claiming to be based upon it – but to complete it – flourish, while the people of the Torah suffered? Why, indeed, ought one to remain a Jew, when every day one was confronted by the success of the daughter religions? Conversion was always a possibility for a member of a despised minority. The search was complicated by the formidable appeal of Greek philosophy to medieval Christian and Islamic civilization. Its rationalism, its openness, its search for pure knowledge challenged all revelations. Philosophy called into question all assertions of truth verifiable not through reason, but only through appeals to a source of truth not universally recognized.

Reason thus stood, it seemed, against revelation. Mysterious divine plans came into conflict with allegations of the limitless capacity of human reason. Free inquiry might lead anywhere and so would not reliably lead to the synagogue, church, or mosque. And not merely traditional knowledge, but the specific propositions of faith and the assertions of a holy book had to be measured against the results of reason. Faith *or* reason – this seemed to be the choice.

For the Jews, moreover, the very substance of faith – in a personal, highly anthropomorphic God who exhibited traits of character not always in conformity with humanity's highest ideals and who in rabbinic hands looked much like the rabbi himself – posed a formidable obstacle. Classical conundrums of philosophy were further enriched by the obvious contradictions between belief in free will and belief in divine providence. The problem of evil remained urgent. And there were other problems. Is God all-knowing? Then how can people be held responsible for what they do? Is God perfect? Then how can he change his mind or set aside his laws to forgive people?

No theologian in such a cosmopolitan, rational age could begin with an assertion of a double truth – one for us, one for them – or a private, relative one. The notion that something could be true for one party and not for another, or that faith and reason were equally valid and yet contradictory, were ideas that had little appeal. And the holy book had to retain the upper hand. Two philosophers represent the best efforts of medieval Judaic civilization to confront these perplexities. Both of them did their work deep within the framework of Rabbinic Judaism and its received canon of law and theology and narrative.

MAIMONIDES

Moses Maimonides (1141–1205) synthesized Aristotelianism with biblical revelation. His *Guide to the Perplexed,* published in 1190, was intended to reconcile the believer to the philosopher and the philosopher to faith. For him philosophy was not alien to religion but identical with it, for truth was, in the end, the sole issue. Faith is a form of knowledge; philosophy is the road to faith. His proof for the existence of God was Aristotelian. He argued from creation to Creator but accepted the eternity of the world. God becomes, therefore, an "absolutely simple essence from which all positive definition is excluded" (Guttmann 1964: 158). One can say nothing about the attributes of God. He is purged of all sensuous elements. One can say only that God is God – nothing more – for God can only be *known* as the highest cause of being.

What then of revelation? Did God not say anything about himself? And if he did, what need for reasonings such as these? For Maimonides, prophecy, like philosophy, depends upon the Active Intellect. Prophecy is a gift bestowed by God upon man. The Torah and commandments are clearly important, but are not ultimately beyond question or reasonable inquiry. They, however, survive the inquiry unimpaired. The Torah fosters a sound mind and body. The greatest good, however, is not to study the Torah in the sense described earlier, but rather to know God – that is, to worship and love him. Piety and knowledge of the Torah serve merely to prepare people for this highest achievement. Study of the Torah loses its character as an end in itself and is rendered into a means to a philosophical goal. This constituted the most striking transformation of the old values (see Box 9.1).

JUDAH HALEVI

Judah Halevi (1080–1141) represents those who found the philosophers presumptuous and incapable of investigating the truths of faith. But the critics of philosophy were themselves philosophers. Halevi produced a set of imaginary dialogues between a king – the King of the Khazars, a kingdom that had, in fact, considered Islam and Christianity and then had adopted Judaism several centuries earlier – in search of true religion and the advocates of the several

BOX 9.1 MAIMONIDES' THIRTEEN PRINCIPLES OF THE FAITH

Maimonides provided a definition of Judaism – a list of articles of faith he thought obligatory on every faithful Jew. These are as follows:

1. existence of God;
2. his unity;
3. his incorporeality;
4. his eternity;
5. the obligation to worship him alone;
6. prophecy;
7. Moses as the greatest of the prophets;
8. the divine origin of Torah;
9. the eternal validity of Torah;
10. God's knowledge of man's deeds;
11. God rewards good and punishes evil;
12. his promise to send a Messiah;
13. his promise to resurrect the dead.

These philosophical principles were hotly debated and much criticized, but, ironically, achieved a place in the life of Judaic piety.

religious and philosophical positions of the day, including Judaism. Judah Halevi, poet and mystic, objected to the indifference of philosophy to the comparative merits of the competing traditions. In philosophy's approach, religion is recommended, but which religion does not matter much. For the majority religions in the West – Islam and Christianity – such an indifference may have been tolerable, but not for a minority destined any day to have to die for the profession of faith.

Martyrdom, such as Jews faced by reason of the Torah, will not be evoked by the unmoved mover, the God anyone may reach either through revelation or through reason. Only for the God of Israel will a Jew give up his or her life. By its nature, philosophy is insufficient for the religious quest. It can hardly compete with – let alone challenge – the *sacred story* of the Jewish people, a history recording extraordinary events starting with revelation. Chapters 2–5 of this book find their place within the mode of exposition portrayed here. What has philosophy to do with Sinai, with the Land, with prophecy?

The Jew expounding religion to the King of the Khazars begins in his own way. It was not like the philosopher with a disquisition on divine attributes, nor like the Christian who starts with the works of creation and expounds the Trinity, nor like the Muslim who acknowledges the unity and eternity of God. Rather it was as follows:

> I believe in the God of Abraham, Isaac, and Israel, who led the Israelites out of Egypt with signs and miracles; who fed them in the desert and gave them the Land, after having made traverse the sea and the Jordan in a miraculous way; who sent Moses with His Torah and subsequently thousands of prophets, who confirmed His law by promises to those who observed and threats to the disobedient. We believe in what is contained in the Torah – a very large domain.
>
> (Heinemann 1960: 33)

The King then asks, "Why did the Jew not say he believes in the creator of the world and in similar attributes common to all creeds?" The Jew responds that the evidence for Israel's faith is *Israel*, the people, this history and endurance, and not the kinds of reasonable truths offered by other traditions. The *proof* of revelation is the testimony of those who were *there* and wrote down what they heard, saw, and did. If so, the King wonders, what accounts for the despised condition of Israel today? The Jew compares Israel to the dry bones of Ezekiel:

> these bones, which have retained a trace of vital power and have once been the seat of a heart, head, spirit, soul, and intellect, are better than bones formed of marble and plaster, endowed with heads, eyes, ears, and all limbs, in which there never dwelt the spirit of life.
>
> (Heinemann 1960: 72)

God's people is Israel; he rules them and keeps them in their present status:

> Israel amid the nations is like the heart amid the organs: It is the most
> sick and the most healthy of them all ... The relationship of the Divine
> power to us is the same as that of the soul to the heart. For this reason
> it is said, "You only have I known among all the families of the earth,
> therefore I will punish you for all your iniquities" (Amos 3:2) ... Now
> we are oppressed, while the whole world enjoys rest and prosperity.
> But the trials which meet us serve to purify our piety, cleanse us, and
> to remove all taint from us.
>
> (Heinemann 1960: 72)

The pitiful condition of Israel is, therefore, turned into the primary
testimony and vindication of Israel's faith. That Israel suffers is
the best assurance of divine concern. The suffering constitutes the
certainty of coming redemption. In the end, the Jew parts from
the King in order to undertake a journey to the Land of Israel. There
he seeks perfection with God. To this the King objects. He thought
the Jew loved freedom, but the Jew finds himself in bondage by
imposing duties obligatory in residing in the Land of Israel. The Jew
replies that the freedom he seeks is from the service of men and the
courting of their favor. He seeks the service of one whose favor is
obtained with the smallest effort: "His service is freedom, and
humility before him is true honor." He, therefore, turns to Jerusalem
to seek the holy life. Here we find no effort to identify Judaism with
rational truth, but rather the claim that the life of the pious Jew
stands above – indeed constitutes the best testimony to – truth.

The source of truth is biblical revelation; it was public, complete,
fully in the light of history. History, not philosophy, testifies to the
truth and in the end constitutes its sole criterion. Philosophy claims
reason can find the way to God. Halevi says only God can show the
way to God, and he does so through revelation, and therefore in
history. For the philosopher, God is the object of knowledge. For
Halevi, God is the subject of knowledge. And Israel has a specifically
religious faculty that mediates the relationship to God; so we have
seen in the references to the role of Israel among the nations as
similar to the role of the heart among the limbs.

Halevi seeks to explain the supernatural status of Israel. The religious faculty is its peculiar inheritance and makes it the core of
humanity. But while the rest of humanity is subject to the laws
of nature, Israel is subject to supernatural, divine providence, mani-

fested in reward and punishment. The very condition of the Jews, in that God punishes them, verifies the particular and specific place of Israel in the divine plan. The teaching of prophecy thus returns in Halevi's philosophy.

These two philosophers were part of a number of important thinkers who attempted to meet the challenge of philosophy and of reason by constructing a comprehensive theological system.

SUBSETS OF RABBINIC JUDAISM: MEDIA OF MYSTICAL PIETY, HASIDISM

Not only did Rabbinic Judaism draw strength from new modes of thought, it also accommodated emphases in piety that placed a higher value on direct encounter with God and on spiritual gifts than, even, upon knowledge of the Torah. The case in point concerns Hasidism, a modern Judaic religious movement.

Beginning in mid-eighteenth-century Ukraine and Poland and continuing to this day as a bastion of true belief and realized Torah piety, Hasidism formed a mystical movement. It drew upon the resources of the Qabbalah, a tradition of mystical doctrine in narrative form that arose in thirteenth-century Spain, and began with emphases quite at variance with those of Rabbinic Judaism. (On Mysticism in Judaism, see Box 9.2.)

What distinguished Hasidism from the standard Rabbinic Judaism was the Hasidic focus on holy men as media of divine grace. These holy men embodied purity and piety. Hasidic groups, taking shape around such charismatic personalities, favored direct encounter with God on the part of holy men. This they chose over meeting God in the Torah on the part of sages.

The mystic circles in Ukraine and Poland in the eighteenth century among whom Hasidism developed carried on certain practices that marked them as different from other Jews – for example, special prayers, distinctive ways of observing certain religious duties, and the like. The first of the movement of ecstatics, Israel b. Eliezer Baal Shem Tov, "the Besht," worked as a popular healer. From the 1730s onward, he undertook travels and attracted to himself circles of followers in Podolia (Ukraine), Poland and Lithuania, and elsewhere. When he died in 1760, he left disciples who organized the movement in southeastern Poland and

BOX 9.2 ABRAHAM JOSHUA HESCHEL'S ACCOUNT OF MYSTICISM IN JUDAISM

The main purpose of mysticism for Judaism is that God is very real, and the desire of the mystic is "to feel and to enjoy Him; not only to obey but to approach Him"; so says Abraham J. Heschel, the greatest theologian of Judaism in the twentieth century, who goes on: "They want to taste the whole wheat of spirit before it is ground by the millstones of reason. They would rather be overwhelmed by the symbols of the inconceivable than wield the definitions of the superficial" (Heschel 1971). What, then, is the mystic doctrine of God in Judaism? This is how Heschel answers that question:

Mystic intuition occurs at an outpost of the mind, dangerously detached from the main substance of the intellect. Operating as it were in no-mind's land, its place is hard to name, its communications with critical thinking often difficult and uncertain and the accounts of its discoveries not easy to decode. In its main representatives, the Kabbalah teaches that man's life can be a rallying point of the forces that tend toward God, that this world is charged with His presence and every object is a cue to His qualities. To the Kabbalist, God is not a concept, a generalization, but a most specific reality; his thinking about Him full of forceful directness. But He who is "the Soul of all souls" is "the mystery of all mysteries." While the Kabbalists speak of God as if they commanded a view of the Beyond, and were in possession of knowledge about the inner life of God, they also assure us that all notions fail when applied to Him, that He is beyond the grasp of the human mind and inaccessible to meditation. He is the *En Sof*, the Infinite, "the most Hidden of all Hidden." While there is an abysmal distance between Him and the world, He is also called All.

For all things are in Him and He is in all things ... He is both manifest and concealed. Manifest in order to uphold the all and concealed, for He is found nowhere. When He becomes manifest He projects nine brilliant lights that throw light in all directions. So, too, does a lamp throw brilliance in all directions, but when we approach the brilliance we find there is nothing outside the lamp.

> So is the Holy ancient One, the Light of all Lights, the most Hidden of all Hidden. We can only find the light which He spreads and which appears and disappears. This light is called the Holy Name, and therefore All is One.

Thus, the "Most Recondite One Who is beyond cognition does reveal of Himself a tenuous and veiled brightness shining only along a narrow path which extends from Him. This is the brightness that irradiates all."

> The *En Sof* has granted us manifestations of His hidden life: He had descended to become the universe; He has revealed Himself to become the Lord of Israel. The ways in which the Infinite assumes the form of finite existence are called *Sefirot*. These are various aspects or forms of Divine action, spheres of Divine emanation. They are, as it were, the garments in which the Hidden God reveals Himself and acts in the universe, the channels through which His light is issued forth.
>
> (Heschel 1971: 284 – 5)

Lithuania. Dov Ber inaugurated the institution of the Hasidic court and dispatched disciples beyond Podolia to establish courts on their own. Most of the major Hasidic circles originate in his disciples. Leadership of the movement passed to a succession of holy men about whom stories were told and preserved. In the third generation, from the third quarter of the eighteenth century into the first of the nineteenth, the movement spread and took hold. Diverse leaders, called *zaddikim*, holy men and charismatic figures, developed their own standing and doctrine.

Given the controversies that swirled about the movement, we should expect that many of the basic ideas would have been new. But that was hardly the case. The movement drew heavily on available mystical books and doctrines, which from medieval times onward had won a place within the faith as part of the Torah as set forth by Rabbinic Judaism. Emphasis on the distinctive doctrines of Hasidic thinkers should not obscure the profound continuities between the modern movement and its medieval sources.

To take one example of how the movement imparted its own imprint on an available idea, Menahem Mendel of Lubavich notes that God's oneness – surely a given in all Judaisms – means more than that God is unique. It means that God is all that is:

There is no reality in created things. This is to say that in truth all creatures are not in the category of something or a thing as we see them with our eyes. For this is only from our point of view, since we cannot perceive the divine vitality. But from the point of view of the divine vitality which sustains us, we have no existence and we are in the category of complete nothingness like the rays of the sun in the sun itself ... From which it follows that there is no other existence whatsoever apart from his existence, blessed be he. This is true unification ...

(Jacobs 1971: 1404)

Since all things are in God, the suffering and sorrow of the world cannot be said to exist. So to despair is to sin.

Hasidism laid great stress on joy and avoiding melancholy. It further maintained that the right attitude must accompany the doing of religious deeds: The deed could only be elevated when carried out in a spirit of devotion. The doctrine of Hasidism moreover held that, "In all things there are 'holy sparks' waiting to be redeemed and rescued for sanctity through man using his appetites to serve God. The very taste of food is a pale reflection of the spiritual force which brings the food into being" (Jacobs 1971: 1405). What followed was that before carrying out a religious deed, the Hasidim would recite the formula, "For the sake of the unification of the Holy One, blessed be he, and his *shekhinah* [presence in the world]." On that account they were criticized. But the fundamental pattern of life, the received worldview contained in the holy canon of Judaism – these defined the issues.

Hasidism, therefore, constituted a Judaic system that took shape within the normative, Rabbinic Judaism – distinctive, yet in its major traits so closely related to Rabbinic Judaism as to be indistinguishable except in trivial details. But one of these mattered a great deal, and that is the doctrine of *zaddikism*: The *zaddik*, or holy man, had the power to raise the prayers of the followers and to work miracles. The *zaddik* was the means through which grace reached the world, the one who controlled the universe through his prayers.

The *zaddik* would bring humanity nearer to God and God closer to humanity. The Hasidism were well aware that this doctrine of the *zaddik* – the pure and elevated soul that could reach to that realm of heaven in which only mercy reigns – represented an innovation. So too did the massive opposition to Hasidism organized by the great sages of the Torah of that time.

By the end of the eighteenth century, powerful opposition, led by the most influential figures of eastern European Judaism, characterized Hasidism as heretical. Its stress on ecstasy, visions, miracles of the leaders, its way of life of enthusiasm, these were seen as delusions, and the veneration of the *zaddik* was interpreted as worship of a human being. The stress on prayer to the denigration of study of the Torah likewise called into question the legitimacy of the movement. In the war against Hasidism, the movement found itself anathematized, its books burned, its leaders vilified. Under these circumstances, the last thing anyone would anticipate would have been for Hasidism to find a place for itself within what would at some point be deemed orthodoxy. But it did.

By the 1830s, the original force of the movement had run its course, and the movement, beginning as a persecuted sect, now defined the way of life of the Jews in the Ukraine, Galicia, and central Poland, with offshoots in White Russia and Lithuania on the one side and Hungary, on the other. The waves of emigration from the 1880s onward carried the movement to the West, and, in the aftermath of World War II, to the U.S.A. and the Land of Israel as well. Today, the movement forms a powerful component of the segregationist-Orthodox Judaism we shall meet in Chapter 10, and that fact is what is central to our interest in the capacity of Rabbinic Judaism to find strength by naturalizing initially alien modes of thought and media of piety. And that is the main point: Rabbinic Judaism possessed the inner resources to make its own what began as a movement of criticism and radical reform of that same Judaism.

RABBINIC JUDAISM DEFINES ITS HERETICS: KARAISM AND SABBATEANISM

If two doctrines characterized normative Rabbinic Judaism they were, first, the doctrine of the dual Torah, written and oral, the oral mediating the written, and, second, the conviction that the Messiah would be a great master of the Torah and would (it hardly needed saying) embody its theology and its law. Both met challenges from Judaic heresies defined within the rabbinic agenda. The first of the two heresies, Karaism, rejected the doctrine of the dual Torah, the second, Sabbateanism, the doctrine of the sage-Messiah.

We look in vain, in the age of the dominance of Rabbinic Judaism, for evidence that the system faced heresies essentially alien to its structure and system. From the fourth to the nineteenth century in Christendom, and to the mid-twentieth century in the Muslim world, Judaic heresies commonly took up a position on exactly the program and agenda of Rabbinic Judaism. What made a heresy heretical, then, was the rejection of one or another of the definitive doctrines of the rabbinic norm.

KARAISM AND THE DOCTRINE THAT AT SINAI GOD REVEALED THE TORAH TO BE TRANSMITTED THROUGH TWO MEDIA, WRITTEN AND ORAL

Focusing upon that central belief, Karaism denied that God revealed to Moses at Sinai more than the written Torah and explicitly condemned belief in an oral one. Karaism rested on four principles: (1) the literal meaning of the biblical text; (2) the consensus of the community; (3) the conclusions derived from Scripture by the method of logical analogy; (4) knowledge based on human reason and intelligence. It took shape in the eighth century, beginning after the rise of Islam, and advocated the return to Scripture as against tradition, inclusive of rabbinic tradition. The sect originated in Babylonia in the period following the formation of the Talmud of Babylonia, on the one side, and the rise of Islam, on the other.

The movement itself claimed to originate in biblical times and to derive its doctrine from the true priest, Zadok. The founder of the movement then recovered that original Torah. The founder, Anan b. David, imposed rules concerning food that were stricter than those of the rabbis, and in other ways legislated a version of the law of a more strict character than the Talmudic authorities admitted. The basic principle predominated that Scriptures were to be studied freely, independently, and individually. No uniformity of view could then emerge. Given the stress of Rabbinic Judaism on the authority of the Talmud and related canonical documents, we could not expect a more precise statement of the opposite view.

We now come to the age in which Rabbinic Judaism in its classical formulation faced competition from Judaic systems that responded to their own urgent questions with their own self-evidently valid answers: New Judaisms.

10

REFORM, ORTHODOX, AND CONSERVATIVE JUDAISMS, ZIONISM

The urgent question that was deemed by many Jews to require an answer shifted in modern times, the eighteenth century to the present. The question "Why is Israel subordinated to the gentiles?" had found its answer in Israel's sanctification and God's judgment for Israel's failures. With the political changes represented by the emancipation of the Jews and their gaining citizenship, a new urgent question arose: How is it possible to be both an Israelite and something else – a French, German, British, or American citizen, for example?

Reform Judaism responded and fixed the pattern of all modern Judaism. It redefined "Israel" to stand for a religious community with a universal mission. It affirmed changes in the way of life and worldview of the received, rabbinic system. These were meant to affirm that the Israelite could integrate and be in addition loyal to France, Britain, Germany, or the U.S.A. Practices that separated the Israelite from the rest of humanity – dietary laws, for example – were to be dropped. Responding to the advent of Reform Judaism, Orthodox Judaism in Germany and the other Western countries rejected the changes Reform made. But Orthodoxy in its integrationist model held that while Judaism endured unchanging, the Israelite should combine study of the Torah with study of secular sciences. So one could both practice Judaism and integrate one's life within the national culture. Conservative Judaism mediated between the two positions, affirming that tradition could change, but only in accord with the historical processes of Judaism over the centuries.

A political, not a religious system, Zionism did not trust the promise of emancipation. It rejected the hope that the Jews could ever be secure in the gentile nations and proposed the creation of a Jewish state in Palestine, where Jews in security could be Jewish and nothing else, for example, speaking Hebrew as their everyday language.

COMPETITION IN DEFINING JUDAISM IN MODERN TIMES

Basic to Judaism from the nineteenth century to the present day has been the division, into distinct movements, of the received Rabbinic Judaism. Of these in the English-speaking world, in the U.S.A., Canada, Britain, and elsewhere, three sizable denominations or movements predominate: Orthodox, Reform, and Conservative Judaism. In North America, approximately half of all Jews affiliated with synagogues identify as Reform, about a third are Conservative, and most of the rest are Orthodox.

To the same circle of new versions of Scripture and tradition belongs Zionism, a political movement aimed at restoring the Jewish people to the Land of Israel, founding the Jewish state, and realizing the nationalism of the Jewish people. Zionism came to fruition in the middle of the twentieth century in the creation of the State of Israel in 1948. These four systems – three religious and Judaic, one political and Jewish – competed productively and continue to thrive. All form mass movements, not just celebrations of particular theologians and their doctrines. All have endured for more than a century.

WHY DID THE RABBINIC SYSTEM MEET COMPETITION?

In the late eighteenth and nineteenth centuries, sweeping changes made urgent political issues that formerly had drawn slight attention.

The Jews had formerly constituted a distinct group. They segregated themselves in culture and ethnic identity and in politics as well. Now in the West they were expected – and aspired – to integrate and form part of an undifferentiated mass of citizens, all of them equal before the law. Jews wanted civil rights and accepted civil obligations of citizenship.

The received Judaism did not address that circumstance. It fostered the self-segregation of the Jews as Holy Israel, their separation from the gentiles in politics and culture, not only in religion. The received system rested on the political premise that God's law formed God's people and governed the Jews. And that sufficed to identify what was meant by "Israel," "a people that dwells apart," in the language of Scripture. The received system did not answer the question, "How can Jews both practice Judaism and also participate in secular society and culture?" None aspired to a dual role. The two political premises – the one of the nation-state, the other of the Torah – scarcely permitted reconciliation.

The consequent Judaic systems, Reform Judaism, a Westernized Orthodoxy that is called integrationist Orthodox Judaism, positive Historical Judaism (in the U.S.A. "Conservative Judaism"), each addressed issues of politics and culture that were regarded as acute and not merely chronic. Reform favored total integration of the Jews into Western culture. Integrationist Orthodoxy concurred but reaffirmed the separateness of Israel, the Holy People, in religious matters. Positive Historical Judaism / Conservative Judaism took the middle position.

The three systems met the political challenge and mediated the cultural ones. All repudiated Judaic self-segregation. Each maintained that Jews could both practice Judaism and serve as good citizens of the nation and participants in the culture of the countries where they found themselves. All alleged that they formed the natural next step in the unfolding of "the tradition," meaning the Judaic system of the dual Torah. Where politics precipitated a new problem, the Judaic systems that emerged responded. In the Russian Empire before Communism (1917), in Russian Poland, White Russia, and Ukraine, Reform, integrationist Orthodox, and Conservative Judaism never registered; the received system continued to answer the urgent questions of the age. No political revolution required change.

REFORM JUDAISM

Reform Judaism (a.k.a. liberal or progressive Judaism) responded to the new questions Jews faced in political emancipation. These changes, particularly in western Europe and the U.S.A., accorded to Jews the status of citizens like other citizens of the nations in which they lived. But they denied the Jews the status of a separate, holy people, living under its own laws and awaiting the Messiah to lead it back to the Holy Land at the end of history. Rather, Reform Judaism looked forward to a messianic age, when the social order would be perfected in justice and humanity, and defined for its "Israel" a mission to hasten the coming of the messianic age. Meanwhile Jews would integrate themselves into the common cultures of the nations where they lived.

Reform Judaism insisted that change in the religion, Judaism, in response to new challenges represented a valid continuation of that religion's long-term capacity to evolve. Reform Judaism denied that any version of the Torah enjoyed eternal validity. All responded to the changes that history brought. Accordingly, Jews should adopt the politics and culture of the countries where they lived, preserving differences of only a religious character, with religion narrowly construed.

CHANGES IN SYNAGOGUE WORSHIP

Reform Judaism finds its beginnings to the nineteenth century in changes, called reforms and regarded as the antecedents of Reform, in trivial aspects of public worship in the synagogue (Petuchowski 1971). The motive for these changes derived from the simple fact that many Jews rejected the received theological system and its liturgical expression. People were defecting from the synagogue. Since it was then taken for granted that there was no secular option, giving up the faith meant surrendering all ties to the group. (Secular Jewish systems, Jewish but not religious, typified by Zionism, emerged only at the beginning of the twentieth century.) The beginning of change addressed two issues at one time: (1) Making the synagogue more attractive so that (2) defectors would return, and others would not leave. The reform of Judaism in its manifestation in synagogue worship – the cutting edge of the faith

– therefore took cognizance of something that had already taken place. And for a sizable sector of Jewry that was the loss for the received system – way of life, worldview, addressed to a defined Israel – of its standing as self-evident truth.

To begin with, the issue involved not politics but merely justification for changing anything at all. The reformers maintained that change was all right because historical precedent proved that change was all right. But change long had defined the constant in the ongoing life of the received Judaism. The normative Judaism endured, never intact but always unimpaired because of its power to absorb and make its own the diverse happenings of culture and society. That fact is established in Chapter 9. Implacable opposition to change represented a change. That was not the real issue. The integration of Israel among the gentiles was.

Reform Judaism affirmed integration and made important changes in the law and theology of Judaism to accommodate it. It did this when the Reform rabbis in the U.S.A. adopted the Pittsburgh Platform of 1885, which stated the Reform system in a clear way (see Box 10.1). The Platform takes up each component of the Reform system in turn. Who is Israel? What is its way of life? How does it account for its existence as a distinct, and distinctive, group?

Israel once was a nation ("during its national life") but today is not a nation. It once had a set of laws that regulate diet, clothing, and the like. These no longer apply, because Israel now is not what it was then. Israel forms an integral part of Western civilization. The reason to persist as a distinctive group was that the group has its work to do, a mission – to serve as a light to the nations. That meant, namely, to realize the messianic hope for the establishment of a kingdom of truth, justice, and peace. For that purpose Israel no longer constitutes a nation. It now forms a religious community.

What that means is that individual Jews do live as citizens in other nations. Difference is acceptable at the level of religion, not nationality, a position that accords fully with the definition of citizenship of the Western democracies. The Reform worldview then lays heavy emphasis on an as-yet-unrealized, but coming, perfect age. Its way of life admits to no important traits that distinguish Jews from others, since morality, in the nature of things, forms a universal category, applicable in the same way to everyone. The theory of Israel then forms the heart of matters, and what we learn

BOX 10.1 THE PITTSBURGH PLATFORM OF REFORM JUDAISM

For Reform Judaism in the nineteenth century, the full and authoritative statement of the system – its worldview, with profound implications on its way of life, and its theory of who is Israel – came to expression in America, in an assembly in Pittsburgh in 1885 of Reform rabbis. At that meeting of the Central Conference of American Rabbis, the Reform Judaism of the age, by now nearly a century old, took up the issues that divided the Judaism and made an authoritative statement on them, one that most Reform Jews could accept. What is important is its formulation of the issue of Israel as political circumstances defined it. Critical to normative Judaism was its view of Israel as God's people, a supernatural polity, living out its social existence under God's Torah. The way of life, one of sanctification, and the worldview, one of persistent reference to the Torah for rules of conduct, on the one side, and of the explanation of conduct, on the other, began in the basic conception of who is Israel. Here too we find emphasis on who is Israel, with that doctrine exposing for all to see the foundations of the way of life and worldview that these rabbis had formed for the Israel they conceived:

> We recognize in the Mosaic legislation a system of training the Jewish people for its mission during its national life in Palestine, and today we accept as binding only its moral laws and maintain only such ceremonies as elevate and sanctify our lives, but reject all such as are not adapted to the views and habits of modern civilization ... We hold that all such Mosaic and rabbinical laws as regular diet, priestly purity, and dress originated in ages and under the influence of ideas entirely foreign to our present mental and spiritual state ... Their observance in our days is apt rather to obstruct than to further modern spiritual elevation ... We recognize in the modern era of universal culture of heart and intellect the approaching of the realization of Israel's great messianic hope for the establishment of the kingdom of truth, justice, and peace among all men. We consider ourselves no longer a nation but a religious community and therefore expect neither a return to Palestine nor a sacrificial worship under the sons of Aaron nor the restoration of any of the laws concerning the Jewish state ...

is that Israel constitutes a "we," that is, that the Jews continue to form a group that, by its own indicators, holds together and constitutes a cogent social entity. All this, in a simple statement of a handful of rabbis, forms a full and encompassing Judaism, one that, to its communicants, presented truth of a self-evident order.

Reform Judaism would evolve beyond the Pittsburgh Platform in the mid-twentieth century, affirming the peoplehood of Israel and renewing received rites. When in 1897 Zionism made its appearance, Reform Judaism rejected it: "Germany is our promised land, and Berlin is our Jerusalem." But by the later 1930s, Reform Rabbis affirmed Zionism. By the twenty-first century, its principles had defined the norm for all communities of Judaism outside the Orthodox framework. It was and remains the most successful Judaic system of modernity. One cannot help admiring the nineteenth-century framers of Reform Judaism for their optimism and their adaptability, their affirmation of progress and their invention of a mission of Israel to help God perfect creation.

But the hopeful version of Reform Judaism would meet its challenge in the Holocaust, and Reform Judaism from World War II onward parted company from its classical formulation in Pittsburgh. Today, Reform Judaism makes provision for religious practices that differentiate Jews from gentiles. It stresses Jewish peoplehood, the ethnic side to things that the founding generations of Reform Judaism relinquished.

INTEGRATIONIST ORTHODOX JUDAISM

The broad category, Orthodox Judaism, requires definition and differentiation. The point of distinction is attitude toward gentile culture. "Integrationist Orthodoxy" differs from "self-segregationist Orthodox."

By "integrationist Orthodox Judaism" in the context of modernizing Judaic systems is meant a very particular approach. It is one that affirms the divine revelation and eternal authority of the Torah, oral and written, *but* that favors the integration of the Jews ("holy Israel") into the national life of the countries of their birth. In cultural terms, this meant study of the Torah and also study of philosophy. I call it "integrationist" for its cultural policy. It also is known as "modern Orthodoxy" or "Western Orthodoxy" or "neo-Orthodoxy."

Other Orthodox communities of Judaism – and they are diverse and many – in common favor the segregation of the holy Israel from other people in the countries where they live, including the State of Israel. Indicators such as clothing, language, above all, education differentiate integrationist from self-segregationist Judaisms. For example, integrationist Orthodoxy holds that secular studies are legitimate, indeed essential, so that Yeshiva University in the U.S.A. and Bar Ilan University in the State of Israel, both successful institutions of integrationist Orthodoxy, offer full academic programs in all sciences and humanities. In them, Judaic religious sciences take cognizance of the challenges of reason and history.

Self-segregated communities of Judaism bear a variety of names, such as traditional, authentic, Haredi (a Hebrew word referring to those that tremble before the Lord), and the like. Self-segregationist Orthodox centers of learning, called *yeshivot*, teach only the sacred sciences, for instance the Talmud and its commentaries. One indicator of the difference between integrationist- and self-segregationist Orthodox Judaisms is the matter of language. The self-segregationists reject the use of Hebrew and preserve Yiddish as the everyday language of the community. Integrationist Orthodoxy in the State of Israel is Hebrew-speaking, like other Israelis. A wide variety of communities of Orthodox Judaism fall into the category of self-segregation. Some are Hasidic, such as we met in Chapter 9, some reject Hasidism and adhere to the classical tradition in all its depth of reason and rationality. But all self-segregated communities of Judaism concur that Holy Israel is not to mix with the gentiles.

Integrationist Jews kept the law of the Torah, for example as it dictated food choices and use of leisure time (to speak of the Sabbath and festivals in secular terms). They sent their children to secular schools, in addition to or instead of solely Jewish ones, or in Jewish schools, they included in the curriculum subjects outside of the sciences of the Torah. In these ways, they marked themselves as integrationist. For the notion that science or German or Latin or philosophy deserved serious study in the nineteenth century struck as wrong those for whom the received system remained self-evidently right. Those Jews did not send their children to gentile schools, and in Jewish schools did not include in the curriculum other than Torah study.

Exactly where and when did integrationist Orthodox Judaism come into being? It was in Germany, in the middle of the nineteenth century, a generation after Reform got going in the same country. Integrationist Orthodoxy responded to the advent of Reform Judaism, which defined the issues of debate. The issues addressed by all parties concerned change and history. The reformers held that Judaism could legitimately change. Judaism was a product of history. The integrationist Orthodox opponents (not to mention the self-segregationist communities of Judaism) denied that Judaism could change. They insisted that Judaism derived from God's will at Sinai and was eternal and supernatural, not historical and man-made. In these two convictions, of course, the integrationist Orthodox recapitulated the convictions of the received system and no one in the self-segregationist Orthodox world would take exception to this position.

Accordingly, the integrationist Orthodox Judaism dealt with the same urgent questions as did Reform Judaism, questions raised by political emancipation. But it gave different answers to them, even though both Reform and integrationist Orthodoxy set forth equally reasoned, coherent theological answers to questions of history and ambient culture. That Orthodoxy maintained the worldview of the received dual Torah, constantly citing its sayings and adhering with only trivial variations to the bulk of its norms for the everyday life. At the same time, integrationist Orthodoxy held, and today holds, that Jews adhering to the dual Torah may wear clothing similar to that which non-Jews wear. The sole exceptions were religious duties not to mix flax and wool (vegetable and animal products woven into cloth), obligatory by the law of the Torah (Lev. 19:19 and Deut. 22:9–11) and to wear show-fringes. They live within a common economy and do not practice distinctively Jewish professions. Many shave and do not grow beards. They take up a life not readily distinguished in important characteristics from the life lived by ordinary people in general.

So for integrationist Orthodoxy, a portion of an Israelite's life may prove secular. The Torah does not dictate and so sanctify all of life's details under all circumstances. The difference between integrationist Orthodoxy and the normative, received system, such as persisted in self-segregationist Judaic circles, therefore comes to expression in social policy: Integration, however circumscribed, versus the total separation of the Holy People from the nations among whom they lived.

Integrationist Judaism thus faced critics in two directions, inside and outside. But it was Reform that precipitated the organization of the integrationist communities of Judaism. Just as the reformers justified change, the integrationist Orthodox theologians denied that change was ever possible. As Walter Wurzburger wrote, "Orthodoxy looks upon attempts to adjust Judaism to the 'spirit of the time' as utterly incompatible with the entire thrust of normative Judaism which holds that the revealed will of God rather than the values of any given age are the ultimate standard" (Wurzburger 1971). To begin with the issue important to the reformers, the value of what was called "emancipation," meaning, the provision to Jews of civil rights, defined the debate. If the Reform made minor changes in liturgy and its conduct, the Orthodox rejected even those that, under other circumstances, might have found acceptance.

Saying prayers in the vernacular, for example, provoked strong opposition. But everyone knew that some of the prayers were said in Aramaic, the vernacular of the ancient Near East. The Orthodox thought that these changes, not reforms at all, represented only the first step of a process leading Jews out of the Judaic world altogether, so, as Walter Wurzburger says, "The slightest tampering with tradition was condemned."

CONSERVATIVE JUDAISM

We treat the German Historical School and Canadian and U.S. Conservative Judaism as a single Judaism, because they share a single viewpoint: Moderation in making change, accommodation between "the tradition" and the requirements of modern life, above all, adaptation to circumstance – all validated by historical research and precedent. The emphasis on historical research in settling theological debates clearly explains the name of the group of German professors who organized the system.

Arguing that its positions represent matters of historical fact rather than theological conviction, the Historical School and Conservative Judaism maintained an essentially secular position. It was that "positive historical scholarship" would prove capable, on the basis of historical facts, of purifying and clarifying the faith, joined to far stricter observance of the law than the reformers required. Questions of theology found their answers in history. Representing in practice a middle position, between integrationist Orthodoxy and Reform, it was in fact an extreme proposition, since it abdicated the throne of theology altogether and established a regency of secular learning. Reform Judaism appealed in the end to systematic religious thinking, while Conservative Judaism accorded an at-best-perfunctory hearing to theological argument and system-building.

The fundamental premise of the Conservatives' emphasis on history rested on the conviction that history and verifiable fact demonstrated the truth or falsity of theological propositions. We should look in vain in all of the prior writings of Judaic systems for precedent for that insistence on critical fact, self-evident to the nineteenth- and twentieth-century system-builders. The appeal to historical facts was meant to lay upon firm, factual foundations whatever change was to take place. In finding precedent for change, the Conservatives sought reassurance that some change – if not a great deal of change – would not endanger the enduring faith they wished to preserve. But there was a second factor. The laws and lessons of history would then settle questions of public policy near at hand.

Both in Germany in the middle of the nineteenth century and in America at the end of the nineteenth century, the emphasis throughout lay on "knowledge and practice of historical Judaism as ordained in the law of Moses expounded by the prophets and sages in Israel in Biblical and Talmudic writings," so the articles of Incorporation of the Jewish Theological Seminary of America Association stated in 1887. Calling themselves "traditionalists" rather than "Orthodox," the conservative adherents accepted for most Judaic subjects the principles of modern critical scholarship. Conservative Judaism therefore exhibited traits that linked it to Reform but also to Orthodoxy, a movement very much in the middle. Precisely how the Historical School related to the other systems of its day – the mid- and later nineteenth century requires attention to that scholarship that, apologists insisted, marked the Historical School off from Orthodoxy.

Not surprisingly, Conservative Judaism derived from professors and relied for its institutions upon academic authority. In the

U.S.A., the head of the organization of Conservative Judaism is the academic chancellor of the Jewish Theological Seminary of America. Maintaining the law and theology of the received Judaism alongside integrationist Orthodoxy, the Historical School, a group of nineteenth-century German scholars, and Conservative Judaism, a twentieth-century mass movement of Judaism in America and Canada, like Reform Judaism, affirmed through secular historical fact the religious legitimacy of change.

The Historical School began among German Jewish theologians who advocated change but found Reform extreme. They parted company with Reform on some specific issues of practice and doctrine, observance of the dietary laws and belief in the coming of the Messiah for example. But they also found the ambient Orthodoxy immobile. Conservative Judaism in America in the twentieth century carried forward this same centrist position and turned a viewpoint of intellectuals into a way of life, worldview, addressed to an Israel. The Historical School, accordingly, shaped the worldview, and Conservative Judaism later on brought that view into full realization as a way of life characteristic of a large group of Jews, nearly half of all American Jews in the middle of the twentieth century, but only a third of American Jewry by the early twenty-first century.

The Historical School in Germany and Conservative Judaism in America affirmed a far broader part of the received way of life than Reform, while rejecting a much larger part than did Orthodoxy of the worldview of the received system. The Historical School concurred with the reformers concerning the norm-setting power of history (Hertzberg 1971). That meant that questions of theology and law could be referred to historians, who would settle matters by appeal to historical precedent. Thus, for example, if one could show that a given law was not practiced prior to a specified period of time, that law could be set aside or modified. If it could be shown, by contrast, that that law goes "way back," then it was treated as sacrosanct. The reformers had held that change was permissible and claimed that historical scholarship would show what change was acceptable and what was not. Concurring in principle, the proponents of the Historical School differed in matters of detail.

Toward the end of the nineteenth century, rabbis of this same centrist persuasion in the U.S.A. organized the Jewish Theological

Seminary of America, in 1886–7, and from that rabbinical school, the Conservative Movement developed. The order of the formation of the several Judaisms of the nineteenth century therefore is, first, Reform, then Orthodoxy, finally, Conservatism – the two extremes, then the middle. Reform defined the tasks of the next two Judaisms to come into being. Orthodoxy framed the clearer of the two positions in reaction to Reform, but, in intellectual terms, the Historical School in Germany met the issues of Reform in a more direct way.

The stress of the Historical School in Europe and Conservative Judaism in America lay on two matters. First, critical scholarship, such as yielded the secular account of the history of Judaism given in Chapter 8, was assigned the task of discovering those facts of which the faith would be composed. Second, Conservative Judaism emphasized the practical observance of the rules of the received Judaism. A fissure opened, then, between scholarship and belief and practice. A professedly free approach to the study of the Torah, specifically through what was called "critical scholarship," would yield an accurate account of the essentials of the faith. But what if that did not emerge? Then the scholars and lay people alike would keep and practice nearly the whole of the tradition just as the Orthodox did.

The ambivalence of Conservative Judaism, speaking in part for intellectuals deeply loyal to the received way of life, but profoundly dubious of the inherited worldview, came to full expression in the odd slogan of its intellectuals and scholars: "Eat kosher and think *traif.*" "Traif" refers to meat that is not acceptable under Judaic law, and the slogan announced a religion of orthopraxy: Do the right thing and it doesn't matter what you believe. That statement meant people should keep the rules of the holy way of life but ignore the convictions that made sense of them. Orthopraxy is the word that refers to correct action and unfettered belief, as against Orthodoxy, right action, and right doctrine. Some would then classify Conservative Judaism in America as an orthoprax Judaism defined through works, not doctrine. Some of its leading voices even denied Judaism set forth doctrine at all; this is called "the dogma of dogmaless Judaism."

What separated Conservative Judaism from Reform was the matter of observance. Fundamental loyalty to the received way of life in the nineteenth and earlier twentieth centuries distinguished the Historical School in Germany and Conservative Judaism in America from Reform Judaism in both countries. When considering the continued validity of a traditional religious practice, the Reform asked "Why?", the Conservatives, "Why not?" The Orthodox, of course, would ask no questions to begin with. The fundamental principle, that the worldview of the Judaism under construction would rest upon (mere) historical facts, came from Reform Judaism. Orthodoxy could never have concurred. The contrast to the powerful faith despite the world, exhibited by integrationist Orthodoxy's stress on the utter facticity of the Torah, presents in a clear light the positivism of the Conservatives, who, indeed, adopted the name "the *positive* Historical School."

But orthopraxy did not yield a stable social order. In America, a pattern developed in which essentially nonobservant congregations of Jews called upon rabbis whom they expected to be observant of the rules of the religion. As a result, many of the intellectual problems that occupied public debate concerned rabbis more than lay people, since the rabbis bore responsibility – so the community maintained – for not only teaching the faith but, on their own, embodying it. An observer described this Judaism as "Orthodox rabbis serving Conservative synagogues made up of Reform Jews."

How do the Reform, integrationist Orthodox, and Conservative systems then compare? Reform identified its Judaism as the linear and incremental next step in the unfolding of the Torah. The Historical School and Conservative Judaism later on regarded its Judaism as the reversion to the authentic Judaism that in time had been lost. Change was legitimate, as the Reform said, but only that kind of change that restored things to the condition of the original and correct Judaism. That position formed a powerful apologetic, because it addressed the Orthodox view that Orthodoxy constituted the linear and incremental outgrowth of "the Torah" or "the tradition," hence, the sole legitimate Judaism. It also addressed the Reform view that change was all right. Conservative Judaism established a firm criterion for what change was all right: The kind that was, really, no change at all. For the premise of the Conservative position was that things should become the way they had always been.

Here we revert to the strikingly secular character of the Reform and Conservative systems: Their insistence that religious belief could be established upon a foundation of historical fact. The category of faith, belief in transcendent things, matters not seen or tangible but nonetheless deeply felt and vigorously affirmed – these traits of religiosity hardly played a role. Rather, fact, ascertained by secular media of learning, would define truth. And truth corresponded to here-and-now reality: How things were. Scholarship would tell how things had always been and dictate those changes that would restore the correct way of life, the true worldview, for the Israel composed of pretty much all the Jews – the center. Historical research therefore provided a powerful apologetic against both sides. Like Orthodoxy, Conservative Judaism defined itself as Judaism, pure and simple. But it did claim to mark the natural next step in the slow evolution of "the tradition," an evolution within the lines and rules set forth by "the tradition" itself.

ZIONISM

Another response to the question of political emancipation, Zionism, founded in Basel, Switzerland, in 1897, constituted the Jews' nationalist movement. Its "Israel" was a nation ("the Jewish people") in quest of a state. It was a secular political movement utilizing the story of Scripture concerning the restoration of Israel, defined as "a People, One People," to the Land of Israel in the end of days. It achieved its goal in the creation of the State of Israel in 1948.

Zionism dismissed the questions answered by Reform and integrationist Orthodox and Conservative Judaisms. Reform Judaism had begun in the premise that the Jews could find a place for themselves in the European nation-states, if they adapted themselves to the duties of shared humanity and a common politics. Integrationist Orthodoxy addressed the same issue. But political anti-Semitism at the end of the nineteenth century – the organization of political parties on a platform of exclusion and repression of the Jews in the European nations – called into question the premises of the Reform and integrationist Orthodox theologians.

It became clear that the Jews, now resident in Europe for more than fifteen centuries, could not hope for the integration they had anticipated at the beginning of the century and for which they had prepared themselves. The urgent question became, "What is to be done to solve what the gentile Europeans called 'the Jewish question'?" Foreseeing exterminationist anti-Semitism, Zionism thus responded to a political crisis, the failure, by the end of the nineteenth century, of emancipation, meaning the promises of political improvement in the Jews' status and condition.

Once more, history defined the arena of contention. To formulate its worldview, Zionism, like Reform Judaism, invented a usable past. Zionism, furthermore, called to the Jews to emancipate themselves by facing the fact that gentiles hated Jews. As to its way of life, Zionism defined itself as the political movement aimed at founding a Jewish state where Jews could free themselves of anti-Semitism and build their own destiny. Activities to secure political support and also persuade the Jewish communities of the need to found a Jewish state formed the way of life.

The Zionist system corresponds in its components to those of Reform and integrationist Orthodoxy: A definition of Israel, a worldview, a way of life (see Box 10.2). Let us therefore turn to the analysis of Zionism viewed within the categories we have used to describe any Judaic system.

For one thing, Zionism enunciated a powerful and original doctrine of Israel. Jews form a people, one people, and should build a nation-state. Given Jews' secular diversity, people could more easily concede the supernatural reading of Judaic existence than the national construction given to it. For, scattered across the European countries as well as in the Muslim world, Jews did not speak a common language, follow a single way of life, or adhere in common to a single code of belief and behavior. What made them a people, one people, and further validated their claim and right to a state, a nation, of their own, constituted the central theme of the Zionist worldview. No facts of perceived society validated that view. In no way, except for a common fate, did Jews form a people, one people. True, in Judaic systems they commonly did. But the received system and its continuators in Reform and integrationist Orthodox Judaisms imputed to Israel, the Jewish people, a supernatural status, a mission, a calling, a purpose. Zionism did not: A people, one people – that is all.

What about its worldview? Zionist theory sought roots for its principal ideas in the documents of the received Judaism, Scripture for example. Zionist theory had the task of explaining how the Jews

BOX 10.2 ZIONISM AND JUDAISM: COMPETING WORLDVIEWS

The Zionist worldview explicitly competed with the religious one. The formidable statement of Jacob Klatzkin (1882 – 1948) provides the solid basis for comparison:

> In the past there have been two criteria of Judaism: The criterion of religion, according to which Judaism is a system of positive and negative commandments, and the criterion of the spirit, which saw Judaism as a complex of ideas, like monotheism, Messianism, absolute justice, etc. According to both these criteria, therefore, Judaism rests on a subjective basis, on the acceptance of a creed ... a religious denomination ... or a community of individuals who share in a *Weltanschauung* ... In opposition to these two criteria, which make of Judaism a matter of creed, a third has now arisen, the criterion of a consistent nationalism. According to it, Judaism rests on an objective basis: To be a Jew means the acceptance of neither a religious nor an ethical creed. We are neither a denomination nor a school of thought, but members of one family, bearers of a common history ... The national definition too requires an act of will. It defines our nationalism by two criteria: Partnership in the past and the conscious desire to continue such partnership in the future. There are, therefore, two bases for Jewish nationalism – the compulsion of history and a will expressed in that history .
>
> (Hertzberg 1971)

formed a people, one people, and in the study of "Jewish history," read as a single, continuous and unitary story, Zionist theory solved that problem. The Jews all came from some one place, traveled together, and were going back to that same one place: One people. Zionist theory therefore derived strength from the study of history, much as had Reform Judaism in its quest to validate change, and in time generated a great renaissance of Judaic studies as the scholarly community of the nascent Jewish state took up the task at hand.

The sort of history that emerged took the form of factual and descriptive narrative. But its selection of facts, its recognition of problems requiring explanation, its choice of what mattered and what did not – all of these definitive questions found answers in the larger program of nationalist ideology. The form was secular and descriptive, but the substance ideological.

At the same time, Zionist theory explicitly rejected the precedent formed by the Torah, selecting as its history not the history of the faith, of the Torah, but the history of the nation, Israel construed as a secular entity. So we find a distinctive worldview that explains a very particular way of life and defines for itself that Israel to which it wishes to speak.

Like Reform Judaism, Zionism found more interesting the written component of the Torah than the Oral; Scripture outweighed the Talmud. And in its search for a usable past, it turned to documents formerly neglected or treated as not authoritative – for instance, the book of Maccabees, a Jewish dynasty that exhibited military prowess. Zionism went in search of heroes unlike those of the present, warriors, political figures, and others who might provide a model for the movement's future, and for the projected state beyond. So instead of rabbis or sages, Zionism chose figures such as David or Judah Maccabee or Samson – David the warrior king; Judah Maccabee, who had led the revolt against the Syrian Hellenists; Samson the powerful fighter.

These provided the appropriate heroes for a political Zionism. The secular system thus proposed to redefine Jewish consciousness, to turn storekeepers into soldiers, lawyers into farmers, corner grocers into builders and administrators of great institutions of state and government. The Rabbinic Judaism had treated David as a rabbi. The Zionist system saw David as a hero in a more worldly sense: A courageous nation-builder.

In its eagerness to appropriate a usable past, Zionism and Israeli nationalism, its successor, dug in the sand to find a deed to the Land. That stress in archaeology on Jewish links to the past extended to even proofs for the biblical record to which, in claiming the Land of Israel, Zionism pointed. So in pre-state times and after the creation of the State of Israel in 1948, Zionist scholars and institutions devoted great effort to digging up the ancient monuments of the Land of Israel, finding in archaeological work the link to the past that the people, one people, so desperately sought.

Archaeology uncovered the Jews' roots in the Land of Israel and became a principal instrument of national expression. Zionism was not alone, for contemporary believers in Scripture archaeology would prove the truths of the biblical narrative. It was not surprising, therefore, that in the Israeli War of Independence, 1948–9, and in later times as well, Israeli generals explained to the world that by following the biblical record of the nation in times past, they had found hidden roads, appropriate strategies – in all, the key to victory.

Why did Zionism succeed where nineteenth-century Reform Judaism gave way? Its advocates claimed that history validated its worldview, way of life, and definition of Israel. From the end of the nineteenth century, Zionism faced political reality and explained it and offered a program, inclusive of a worldview and a way of life, that worked. At the end of World War II, with millions murdered, as Zionism had predicted they would be, Zionism offered Jewry the sole meaningful explanation of how to endure. Zionism had led at least some Zionists to realize as early as 1940 what Hitler's Germany was going to do. At a meeting in December 1940, Berl Katznelson, an architect of Socialist Zionism in the Jewish community of Palestine before the creation of the State of Israel, announced that European Jewry was finished:

> The essence of Zionist awareness must be that what existed in Vienna will never return, what existed in Berlin will never return, nor in Prague, and what we had in Warsaw and Lodz is finished, and we must realize this! Why don't we understand that what Hitler has done, and this war is a kind of Rubicon, an outer limit, and what existed before will never exist again ... And I declare that the fate of European Jewry is sealed.
>
> (Shapira 1974).

Zionism, in the person of Katznelson, even before the systematic mass murder got fully underway, grasped that, after World War II, Jews would not return to Europe, certainly not to those places in which they had flourished for 1,000 years, and Zionism offered the alternative: The building, outside of Europe, of the Jewish state. So Zionism took a position of prophecy and found its prophecy fulfilled. Its fundamental dogma about the character of the diaspora as exile found verification in the destruction of European Jewry. And Zionism's further claim to point the way forward proved to be Israel's salvation in the formation of the State of Israel on the other side of the Holocaust. So Katznelson maintained: "If Zionism wanted to be the future force of the Jewish people, it must prepare to solve the Jewish question in all its scope" (Shapira 1974: 290).

The secret of the power of Zionism lay in its power to make sense of the world and to propose a program to solve the problems of the age. That same power animated Reform, integrationist Orthodox, and Conservative Judaisms.

PART IV

THE HOLOCAUST

11

HOW JUDAISM SPEAKS TODAY

The Holocaust forms the single paramount topic of Judaic public discussion today and will continue to dominate for the foreseeable future. A Judaic system, the Judaism of Holocaust and Redemption, today joins the Holocaust to the creation of the State of Israel. It links the secular and the theological, the Israeli and the diaspora communities of Judaism.

But the Judaism of Holocaust and Redemption has not silenced normative theological discussion in Judaism. When we set Orthodox and Reform statements not about but of Judaism side by side, the two transmit a coherent message, an ongoing story in common. The messages of the competing Judaic systems, moreover, intersect and differ only in trivial ways.

Basic Judaism continues to sustain creative theology and the Torah to shape the mind of the contemporary communities of Judaism.

THE JUDAISM OF HOLOCAUST AND REDEMPTION

The Judaism of Holocaust and Redemption is a Jewish cultural system that focuses upon (1) the murder of nearly 6 million European Jews in 1933–45, in connection with World War II, by the

Germans and their allies, that is, the Holocaust, and (2) the creation of the State of Israel seen as the consequence of the Holocaust, that is, Redemption. The system as a whole presents an encompassing story, linking one event to the other as an instructive pattern. It moves Jews to follow a particular set of actions, rather than other sorts. It compellingly answers urgent questions of contemporary Jews both in the State of Israel and in the Diaspora.

The ancient pattern of exile and return again is realized. The exile part here refers to the mass murder of most of Europe's Jews. The return part comes in the restoration of Israel to the Land of Israel and creation of the State of Israel. This system tells ethnic Jews who they are, why they should be Jewish, what they should do because of that mode of identification. Ethnic Jews are all those who would have been put to death had they lived in World War II Europe, that is, those with a single Jewish grandparent. They should be Jewish to keep their group alive despite the best efforts of their enemies to annihilate them. What they should do because of their ethnic affiliation is remember the Holocaust and support the State of Israel. It goes without saying, Holocaust and Redemption also explain who the Jewish group is and how that group should relate to the rest of the world and to history.

The system of Holocaust and Redemption today dominates the realm of secular Jewishness. It forms the rationale for organized Jewish community activities and programs. The State of Israel seen in the setting of the Holocaust and its aftermath forms the principal focus of ethnic commemoration and celebration.

The Judaic system of Holocaust and Redemption today pervades Reform and Conservative Judaism in North America. That is shown by a simple fact. "Jewish survival" forms the goal and rationale for their programs, to which the classical expressions of piety, prayer, and Torah study are tangential. Integrationist Orthodoxy too is deeply devoted to the Land and affirms the State of Israel as a chapter in the messianic drama of restoration of Israel to the Land of Israel. (This religious reading of the State of Israel as a chapter in the messianic drama will become clear in the remarkable statement of Rabbi Avi Shafran cited later on in this chapter.) Self-segregationist Orthodoxy is divided on the subject. Some Hasidic and *yeshiva*-centered non-Hasidic groups recognize the State in a secular framework but do not identify it with the advent of the messianic age. A few minor Hasidic communities reject the State of Israel out of hand and do not recognize it in any positive light.

That amalgamation of a secular and a theological system contradicts our starting point, the distinction between religiosity and ethnicity among Jews. For purposes of describing basic Judaism, we separated the ethnic group, the Jews, and the religious community, the community of Judaism. That distinction depended upon our constructing an ideal type. We therefore set aside nuance and detail in favor of an explicit focus on the religious system, Judaism, as set forth in its canonical writings and by authoritative representatives. Furthermore, that same distinction between ethnic opinion and religious doctrine made possible describing Judaism without constant reference to what "the Jews" – some of them secular to the core – believe. So Judaism to this point has not found its definition in Jewish public opinion polling but in widely told stories.

But when it comes to the system of Holocaust and Redemption, we find a secular narrative dominant in contemporary religious systems of Judaism. The story that is told by the Judaism before us dominates in the narratives of Reform and Conservative and integrationist Orthodox Judaisms. It infuses their worldview, treating as subordinate the established stories of Creation and the Exodus from Egypt and the like. It is of this world and its narrative does not compare in depth or density with the stories of Creation, the patriarchs and matriarchs, the Exodus from Egypt, the Torah of Sinai, or the exile and return of prophetic testimony before and after 586 B.C.E. More to the point, the narratives of Holocaust and Redemption and of Creation and Exodus and Sinai scarcely intersect. Yet one and the same communities of Judaism tell the distinct stories, so different in character and content. The theological consequences will emerge when we revert to the problem of evil, raised in radical form by the Holocaust but not resolved by the creation of the State of Israel.

THE WORLDVIEW, WAY OF LIFE, AND THEORY OF ISRAEL OF THE JUDAISM OF HOLOCAUST AND REDEMPTION

The ethnic-Jewish framing of the worldview stresses the unique character of the murder of European Jews and the providential and redemptive meaning of the creation of the State of Israel.

Sanctification of everyday life through obedience to divine imperatives – commandments – does not figure.

Synagogues with their program of prayer, Torah study, and celebration take a tangential position. They are enlisted in Holocaust
Memorial projects – memorial services for example – but do not
take a position that is critical to the worldview of that system. What
of the other half, the redemption part? Synagogue support for the
State of Israel is taken for granted, for example, through political
activity. A way of life particular to the synagogue is difficult to
identify in the system of Holocaust and Redemption. One need not
belong to a synagogue in order to participate in the system of
Holocaust and Redemption. But synagogue Jewry affirms the self-
evident validity of that system.

The system's way of life requires active work in raising money
and political support for the State of Israel and engagement with
telling the story of the Holocaust. It fosters building Holocaust
Memorials – museums – in the Diaspora and paying visits to
Auschwitz and to Masada, the site in the Land of Israel where the
last stand against Rome in 73 C.E. ended in mass suicide.
Educational projects in public schools, attendance at films on the
theme of the Holocaust, attending rites of remembrance – these
form the way of life of the secular system. The holy day of the
Judaism of Holocaust and Redemption is not the ninth of Ab,
commemorating catastrophes through time, as we shall see, but
Holocaust Memorial Day, a special occasion.

The urgent question answered by the system of Holocaust and
Redemption is, "Why should Jews be Jewish?" And the self-evident
answer is, "To continue the ethnic group that the Holocaust nearly
wiped out, especially through the State of Israel, which is Jewry's
answer to the Holocaust." The survival for its own sake, not for
God's sake, of Israel the people, has no precedent in prior Judaic
systems. The creed begins with the resolve "not to hand Hitler any
more victories." He wanted to wipe out the Jewish people, so he is
defeated when Jews affirm being Jewish. What that affirmation
entails proves remarkably vague.

Different from Zionism, which held that "Israel" means only the
State of Israel and that Jews legitimately can live a full Jewish life
only in the Jewish state, this system serves, in particular, to give
Jews living in America, Canada, Britain and elsewhere in the

Diaspora a secular reason and an ethnic explanation for being Jewish. It forms the bridge between them and the State of Israel, affording them a stake in the State. And, most strikingly, while the Judaism of the dual Torah infused the everyday life of the faithful with divine imperatives of sanctification, the Judaism of Holocaust and Redemption made few concrete demands on its Israelites, except in the shaping of attitudes.

THE PROBLEM OF EVIL

The Judaism of Holocaust and Redemption keeps silent on the problem of evil. With the events of the Holocaust, however, the problem of evil moves from chronic to acute status: "Where was God in Auschwitz?" But that is the case mainly with a handful of theologians (see Rubenstein 1966). The full secularity of the Judaism of Holocaust and Redemption is measured by the absence of theological debate among its intellectual leaders, novelists and historians and politicians but only occasional theologians.

Prior calamities, from ancient Israelite times forward, precipitated self-incrimination: "On account of our sins we have been exiled from our land" expresses the norm, and makes its appearance in the Sabbath liturgy. That articulates the classical theology of divine justice. The destruction of the Temple brought about extensive soul-searching.

None of these normative attitudes of Rabbinic Judaism surfaced where the Judaism of Holocaust and Redemption predominated. Reform, integrationist Orthodoxy, and Conservative Judaism have not explored the issue but suppressed it. It is difficult to locate in the history of Judaism a counterpart response to catastrophe, one that did not call for repentance and atonement for the sin that has brought disaster (see Kraemer 1995). Understandably, few theologians explored the classic response to the problem of evil, and those that did got no hearing. For who could aver that the millions who died, died for their sins? On the other hand, and more telling still, none invoked the coming judgment and the Resurrection of the Dead, even though these convictions formed the foundation of daily prayer.

The classical problem is easily reprised. If God is all-powerful, he cannot also be deemed merciful, for where was his love for the million Jewish children who were murdered in the Holocaust? And if God is merciful, he cannot be deemed powerful, for he did not prevent mass murder. And to speak of "justice" and "Holocaust" in the same breath stifles all rationality. The problem of evil, unique to monotheism for reasons set forth in Chapter 7, for long centuries occupied prophets and sages, theologians and philosophers alike. The question of why the wicked prosper and the righteous suffer, we recall, troubled Jeremiah and preoccupied the author of Job. The rabbinic sages worked on the issue and produced a coherent response. There is no problem of evil because God ultimately will justly judge all humanity and will raise from the dead those that merit resurrection. So the fate of humanity in the end does not lead to the grave but provides in the afterlife a just outcome for wicked and righteous alike.

But in the aftermath of the Germans' war against the Jews, the classical response to crisis has rarely found its hearing. No theologian writing in English invoked the Resurrection of the Dead to resolve the problem. Instead, as we have seen, an essentially secular and this-worldly system predominated. No one can predict the future.

HOW JUDAISM SPEAKS TODAY

Basic Judaism today, as in the past, finds its voice in telling the ongoing story and practice of Judaism. Normative Judaism – the Judaism of Scripture, Mishnah, Talmud, Midrash, and tradition – speaks today exactly as it has spoken for millennia. That is through expositions of the Torah set forth by learned rabbis.

The idiom has changed. The message endures. Not intact but ever unimpaired, the tradition gains strength. No account of the basics of Judaism can complete its picture without a clear statement of how the contemporary practice of Judaism encompasses that very same Torah that has set forth the Judaic narrative from the beginning.

Two examples of contemporary Judaic discourse serve. They come from the extremes, one by an Orthodox rabbi who in public discourse of Judaism represents a community of self-segregationist Orthodox Judaism, the other by a Reform rabbi who is a professor at Hebrew Union College – Jewish Institute of Religion, in New York City, the Reform Rabbinical Seminary. The two represent extremes of contemporary Judaism, self-segregationist Orthodoxy against Reform Judaism. They have in common the remarkable capacity to speak to time from eternity.

The first addresses a crisis of faith because of a specific political event in the State of Israel, the evacuation of Jewish settlements in Gaza in the summer of 2005. He shows how the received tradition responds to events of the hour. The second expounds an enduring rite and its contemporary implications for morality. He brings the received tradition to the contemporary world. The paradox is that the Orthodox voice addresses the ephemeral world of politics, and the Reform voice captures the natural sounds of the tradition. Yet they converge. First, they build upon the same premises. Second, they deliver a single message in common. They justify regarding Judaism as a coherent religious system, even while we take account of variations.

To be sure, for both, like the destruction of the Temple in 70 C.E., the Holocaust forms the background for the contemporary encounter with God in the Torah. But it does not dominate the agenda. And the Torah's story governs and finds a place, also, for the contemporary event.

Because of their power to exemplify how Judaism speaks today, I cite the complete statements. The main criterion for selection is excellence in showing how the classical Torah and its received commentaries shape contemporary discourse. For Judaism in the English language, many qualified rabbis present worthy choices. Finding the relevance of enduring truths to contemporary dilemmas defines the task of the rabbi. The two at hand illustrate the eloquence and theological profundity in the encounter with the Torah exhibited by today's voices of Judaism.

AN ORTHODOX VOICE

Writing in the *New York Jewish Week* and in numerous other English-language Jewish community newspapers throughout the U.S.A. and Canada, Rabbi Avi Shafran is Director of Public Affairs for Agudath Israel of America, an organization of Orthodox Judaism founded in post World War I Poland to speak for the community of the Torah. Agudath Israel began in the *yeshivah* world that rejected both political Zionism and the integrationist Orthodoxy of Western Europe and the U.S.A.

Rabbi Shafran here represents the Torah without stipulation or apology. He addresses the Israeli evacuation of the Jewish community of the Gaza Strip in the summer of 2005 and shows how acutely contemporary issues come under the perspective of the Torah. That is what recommends his eloquent essay.

Specifically, he makes reference to the ninth of Ab, the day of mourning for calamities in the history of the Jewish people.

Mishnah-tractate Taanit 4:5

A. Five events occurred to our fathers on the seventeenth of Tammuz, and five on the ninth of Ab.

B. On the seventeenth of Tammuz [26b] the tablets [of the Torah] were broken, the daily whole offering was canceled, the city [wall] was breached, Apostemos burned the Torah, and he set up an idol in the Temple.

C. On the ninth of Ab the decree was made against our forefathers that they should not enter the land, the first Temple and the second [Temple] were destroyed, Betar was taken, and the city was ploughed up [after the war of Hadrian].

He shows how Judaic theology links the immediate moment to the long memory invoked by that day of mourning. He finds a place for what is new within the pattern established as true. That is how Orthodoxy conveys the Judaism of the hour. But in a moment we shall see no less in Reform Judaism, rather, examples of that same capacity to find in the Torah an authentic divine message for today.

Here is how the hope for the coming of the Messiah and the end of days takes up a critical position in Judaic response to a crisis of the hour. The concluding lines capture that hope in its fullness (see Box 11.1).

The message of Rabbi Shafran transcends the politics and issues of public policy that predominate in the discussion of the State of Israel in relationship to Palestine. Note the immediate recourse to the Torah, here to the ninth of Ab. Do not miss the reference to synagogue liturgy, the seamless web that through all time joins the practice of Judaism to its theological foundations. That is what defines contemporary Judaic theological discourse, the ability to

BOX 11.1 GAZA, INTERRUPTED

Gaza will soon be empty of Jews. Whether the decision to render it so was wisdom or folly, whether it marked the beginning of a more stable Middle East or a more volatile one, whether it served to empower Palestinians considered moderate or to encourage those proven to be murderous are questions now being addressed with passion. History will one day address them with hindsight.

But the human tragedy of the withdrawal is undeniable. Those of us who have never been compelled to leave our homes, the fields we planted and harvested, the synagogues in which we prayed and studied, the cemeteries in which our loved ones are buried, cannot claim to truly appreciate the agony of those who lived in Gaza, and now no longer do. Those displaced families, noble and loving of the land, deserve our deepest sympathy and concern.

Concern for the future, though, is called for, too. Relinquishing territory to at best an unproven entity trying to govern a populace that embraces wild-eyed killers is not an obviously healthy thing, to put it delicately. Yet, despite it all, what no believing Jew may feel in the wake of the Gaza withdrawal is despair. Traumas like that of the past weeks should never be permitted to obscure a larger picture, the true one. It is a picture well framed by its timing.

Events in Gaza reached their crescendo and denouement at an appropriate season of the Jewish year: The mournful days leading up to Ninth of Ab, and then, that sorrowful day itself. Equally apt, though, was – and is – the assurance of Jewish tradition that, in the dark damp of Ninth of Ab's tragedy, the seeds of Jewish redemption quietly sprout.

A believing Jew recognizes that unfortunate things, even tragic things, happen, that many are the prayers denied. Moses, as Jews the world over recently read in the Sabbath portion, was not granted his yearning to walk on the soil of the Holy Land; the "generation of the desert" was fated the same. Jewish history, even after the Temples' destructions and the Jewish exile from the Holy Land, has been replete with deep disappointments and worse – crusades, pogroms, blood libels and expulsions. And here we sit, just over a half-century removed from the annihilation of eastern European Jewry.

And yet where we sit, too, is amid an abundance of spiritual resurgence. Whatever problems may plague the contemporary Jewish world, the reestablishment, in Israel and worldwide, of the Jewish learning and life that once epitomized European Jewry is astounding – and a vital lesson about the permanence of God's love for His people.

Beating with that lesson, the hearts of believing Jews discern things beyond the nonce; here, beyond the Gaza withdrawal. True, the State of Israel may be smaller than it was last month, but Eretz Yisrael, the land bequeathed the Jewish people, has not shrunk in the least. Part of it may be lonelier now, but it will be patient; its rightful residents will return one day. Yes, sworn enemies of the Jewish people are now closer to Jewish cities, but Jewish lives remain, as always, in the hands of our Protector; if we merit His protection, the only victims of suicide bombers will be themselves.

And while members of Hamas may chant and fire weapons to mark what they perceive as a victory, and recommit themselves to their gleeful blood lust, a believing Jew knows that one day there will be another festivity, infinitely greater, a celebration of the utter downfall of those barbarians and all their supporters. And it then will be the Jewish people and the righteous among the nations who will exult, singing praises, not firing guns.

What will bring about that ultimate rejoicing, the return of all of the Holy Land to its rightful heirs and the banishment of evil from humanity, will not be, in the sardonic words of the prophet, "my strength and the power of my hand" – neither geopolitical machinations nor advanced weaponry. What will bring it about will be something else entirely, something that was ironically evident – the seeds in the darkness – amid the turmoil of the withdrawal itself.

The media were filled with the predictable images of confrontation – the ugliest, products of radical youths that arrived in Gaza from elsewhere. There were even some Jews, elsewhere, who, tragically, seemed to adopt the methods and madness of our enemies.

More telling, though, were many other scenes, poignant ones of soldiers and residents in heartfelt conversations, embracing each other, comforting one another, crying together. A local family offering a hot soldier a drink, a soldier kissing the Torah that a rabbi was evacuating from a synagogue. The images were of siblings on opposite ends of a difficult situation not of their making, not in their control.

Those images hold the keys to the Jewish future, to the redemption that believing Jews know will in time arrive. We cannot hasten it with some Jewish *jihad*, nor with trust in political or military leaders or tactics. We hurry it only with Jewish observance, Jewish study, Jewish tears, Jewish love.

The seven weeks that follow the ninth of Ab are known in Jewish tradition as the "Seven Weeks of Comforting." They are a time for remembering God's promise that although Jewish tragedy may seem overwhelming, redemption will in time arrive. And when it does, the Jewish land, all of it, will rejoice beyond imagining with its rightful inhabitants.

Rabbi Avi Shafran

treat the present moment within the analogy of the established pattern, to interpret today in light of eternity.

What is striking in Rabbi Shafran's message is the power of the Torah – the ninth of Ab here – to accommodate what is new and unique. That is not merely to make a point of history, but to establish a truth of faith: "the assurance of Jewish tradition that, in the dark damp of Ninth of Ab's tragedy, the seeds of Jewish redemption quietly sprout." Rabbi Shafran encompasses the Holocaust in this tragic vision, an event in a long list of similar events. But he finds hope in the renewal of Israel the Jewish People and the Torah as the source of renaissance: "Whatever problems may plague the contemporary Jewish world, the reestablishment, in Israel and worldwide, of the Jewish learning and life that once epitomized European Jewry is astounding – and a vital lesson about the permanence of God's love for His people." The ultimate message is one of faith in God.

The redemption can be brought nearer: "We hurry it only with Jewish observance, Jewish study, Jewish tears, Jewish love."

Rabbi Shafran could well have spoken as a rabbi addressing Jewry in the aftermath of the Crusaders' mass murders of the Jews in the Rhineland in the eleventh century. The message is the same. Only the setting has changed.

A REFORM VOICE

What is striking in the Sabbath-lection essays of Rabbi Lawrence A. Hoffman, Professor of Liturgy at the Reform rabbinical school, Hebrew Union College – Jewish Institute of Religion in New York City, is his classicism. Writing for a mass audience, also like Rabbi Shafran in the *New York Jewish Week*, Rabbi Hoffman's mode of argument, his choice of proof-texts, the connections he draws and the metaphors he devises, his approach to the exposition of Scripture for a contemporary audience – his voice is indistinguishable from that of any literate Orthodox Rabbi of the same time and place. I reproduce one of his weekly columns, to show the consistency of his definition of Torah study as source of compelling theology of Judaism.

Rabbi Hoffman builds a bridge between details of the text and the community that receives the text as "the Torah that God set before Israel through the intervention of Moses." Here is his comment on the Torah-lection that presents the law (see Box 11.2).

The story of Scripture forms the implicit foundation of this lesson. And that story establishes the location and the lesson: Secular and sacred, synagogue and temple. Notice how the topic attracts comment over the ages, even stimulating the great Maimonides to clarify the details. And see how deftly Rabbi Hoffman shifts the discussion from the temple of Jerusalem to the existential issue at hand: Are you allowed to enjoy yourself, if the enjoyment is not connected to the sanctuary? The answer is "Yes, but ... " Then comes the bridge to today: "The 'But ... ' is the warning against cutting oneself off from the sacred altogether. Still using the metaphor of food, our *sedra* [lection] addresses the cautionary 'But ... ' by demanding a unique kind of tithe."

That leads to the lesson for today: If we do not regularly reconnect with the sacred, we will come to believe that the sacred does

BOX 11.2 PARASHAT RE'EH

In this final and retrospective book of Torah, we expect such things as the Ten Commandments reiterated, and (eventually) the death of Moses. But who would have predicted Deuteronomy 12:20: "When God expands your territory and you find yourself hungry for meat, you may eat it anytime you want."

The issue is *besar ta'avah* (as the Talmud calls it), meat unconnected to sacrifice, and eaten just because it tastes good. We mistakenly think of sacrifices as belonging to God. But many offerings, though slaughtered in the tabernacle (later, the temple), were consumed by the people bringing them. On Passover, for example, thousands descended upon Jerusalem with lambs for slaughter.

In the wilderness, says the Ramban (Maimonides), everyone's tent was pitched within an easy walk of the tabernacle. Whoever yearned for steak took an animal to the sanctuary, slaughtered it there, and carried it home to dinner. Once in the Land, however, the far-flung population (even in Jerusalem itself) could hardly take animals to the temple before eating them. So the question arose as to whether they might eat non-sacrificial meat, and the answer, we learn now, is, "Yes."

The question should interest everyone, not just carnivores, because it illustrates a deeper challenge: How to pursue a sacred life far away from the sacred. Wilderness living was like a tiny village, where every moment of everyone's day revolved about God's everyday presence in the tabernacle. From Joshua on, however, it was possible for most people never to know that ineffable sense of the sacred. Hence the question: "Are you allowed to enjoy yourself, if the enjoyment is not connected to the sanctuary?" The answer is "Yes, but ... "

The "But ... " is the warning against cutting oneself off from the sacred altogether. Still using the metaphor of food, our *sedra* [lection] addresses the cautionary "But ... " by demanding a unique kind of tithe.

We think of tithing as moneys given to others, usually our religious institutions, and indeed, one biblical tithe is just that: It goes to the temple Levites who share it with the priests. But there are two other tithes as well. The years are grouped into sevens. Every seventh year is a sabbatical when the land lies fallow; in the third and sixth years of the seven-year cycle, a "poor person's tithe" goes to feed the indigent; in every first, second, fourth and fifth year, a tithe of food is set aside for the owners themselves to eat on a pilgrimage to Jerusalem. If you live so far away that your food would spoil en route, you trade it in for a wad of money that you take to Jerusalem, to buy "cattle, sheep, wine, liquor, or whatever else you desire" (Deut. 14:25). This is a tithe? It sounds more like an excuse for a wild party.

It actually is that, the point being to make people party in Jerusalem, the sacred soil of the city of David and the temple itself, where, like the desert sanctuary, God establishes a presence. If we do not regularly reconnect with the sacred, we will come to believe that the sacred does not exist.

Isn't that our problem too? How sacred is the Long Island Railroad, or a home in Harrison, Hoboken, or the Upper West Side? We live, work, and play entirely in the realm of the secular. Can we even imagine a tabernacle or temple towering over us?

Tradition answers the problem with the synagogue. In theory, attending a synagogue dinner ought to be like eating our tithes in Jerusalem; attending services should be like standing in the temple courtyard. So why doesn't it?

The sad truth is our synagogues too have gone secular. We treat religious school like PS 102: Drop kids off; make sure they pass. We *daven* properly, pray with propriety – never mind spirituality. We have meetings there too: Business meetings, like those we conduct at work (except, maybe, less efficient). "Efficient?" There's a concept straight out of secularity. Traveling forty years in the wilderness was inefficient; so too was the route from Egypt, which meandered needlessly (from the viewpoint of efficiency) all through Sinai instead of hugging the Mediterranean coast.

Passing, propriety, and efficiency are secular categories. Imagine services where we really feel blessed; synagogue schools where kids know God; and meetings governed by God's, not Robert's, rules of order.

Secularity is fine: Like *besar ta'avah*, it is ours for the asking. But satisfying secular tastes eventually pales. We need synagogues that feel sacred to recommit us to the task of being Israel, agents of God's presence among the nations. Does your synagogue provide that certainty? It can, and it should. If it doesn't, write a secular letter to your rabbi and congregational president to ask why not.

Rabbi Lawrence A. Hoffman

not exist. And that leads to the point of it all: The secularization of the synagogue. And the point of it all is the "task of being Israel." It is difficult to find a word in this lesson that Rabbi Shafran would not approve.

For the English-speaking world of Judaism Rabbis Shafran and Hoffman attest to what is basic in Judaism, pure and simple.

GLOSSARY AND ABBREVIATIONS

Abot Tractate of the Mishnah, "The Fathers," contains wise sayings of ancient sages.

Abot de R. Natan The Fathers According to Rabbi Nathan, a commentary to tractate Abot.

Akedah the Binding of Isaac, as narrated in Genesis 22.

Alenu "Let us praise him," the closing prayer of Jewish worship.

Aqedah *see* Akedah.

Aramaic a Semitic language, widely spoken in the Near and Middle East in antiquity. It replaced Hebrew in Israelite usage in ancient times.

Ashkenazi a Jew who originates in central or eastern Europe.

B. Bavli, Talmud of Babylonia, produced in the Iranian Empire, in the province of Babylonia (roughly in the area of present-day Baghdad) in *c.* 600 C.E.

Bavli the Talmud of Babylonia.

B.C.E. Before the Common Era (B.C.).

Berit covenant.

Berit Milah covenant of circumcision.

Binding of Isaac the narrative of Genesis 22.

Birkat Hammazon *see* Grace after Meals.

C.E. Common Era (A.D.).

Constantine Roman emperor who in 312 C.E. declared Christianity a licit religion.

Dan. Daniel.

Day of Atonement Yom Kippur, fast day on the tenth of the lunar month of Tishré, for confession and forgiveness of sins.

Days of Awe the ten days beginning with Rosh Hashanah, the New Year, the first day of the lunar month of Tishré, and ending with Yom Kippur, the tenth day of that same month; the season when all persons are judged for their deeds in the past year and recorded for the year to come.

Deut. Deuteronomy.

Diaspora dispersion, refers to Jews living outside of the Land of Israel.

Dual Torah the Torah in two media, writing and memory; the written part is equivalent to the books of the Hebrew Scriptures, a.k.a. the Old Testament. The oral part originated in a chain of tradition from master to disciple, beginning with God and Moses at Sinai, and is now recorded in the rabbinical writings of the first six centuries C.E., from the Mishnah to the Bavli.

eschatological having to do with the end of history, the theory of last things.

ethical monotheism belief that there is only one God, who is all-powerful, just and merciful and who binds himself to do justice.

ethics the worldview of a religious system of the social order.

ethnos the identification and definition of the community that embodies a religious system of the social order.

ethos the way of life of a religious system of the social order.

exile Jews living outside of the Land of Israel.

Exod. Exodus.

Ezek. Ezekiel.

Fathers According to Rabbi Nathan *see* Abot de R. Natan.

Galut the situation of being in exile.

Gen. Genesis.

Gen. R. *see* Genesis Rabbah.

Genesis Rabbah Rabbinic commentary to the book of Genesis, came to closure at *c.* 450 C.E.

Golah exile, the situation of Jews who live outside of the Land of Israel.

Grace after Meals formal prayer at the conclusion of a meal that has begun with a *motzi; see motzi.*

Haggadah narrative; especially Passover narrative.

Holocaust the murder of nearly 6 million Jews by Germany between 1933 and 1945.

Hos. Hosea.

huppah marriage canopy.

huts tabernacles, flimsy dwellings, partially open to the sky, where Israelites take up residence for the Festival of Tabernacles. Hebrew: *sukkah, sukkot* (pl.).

Is. Isaiah.

Jer. Jeremiah.

Jewishness the ethnic culture of the Jews as a secular group.

Josh. Joshua.

Judaism a religious system of ethical monotheism that privileges the Pentateuch.

Judaism of the Dual Torah the Judaic religious system that holds God revealed the Torah to Moses at Sinai in two media, writing and memory, a.k.a. Rabbinic Judaism.

Judaist a practitioner of a Judaism.

Julian Roman emperor, who in 361 C.E. announced that the Jews may rebuild the temple of Jerusalem; died soon afterward, and nothing came of it.

Kgs. Kings.

Lam. Lamentations.

Lam. R. Lamentations Rabbah, a rabbinic commentary to the book of Lamentations.

Lev. Leviticus.

Lev. R. Leviticus Rabbah, a rabbinic commentary to the book of Leviticus, *c.* 450 C.E.

Makkot Mishnah-tractate on the topic of the penalty of flogging.

Mekhilta Attributed to R. Ishmael a rabbinic commentary to the book of Exodus.

Midrash interpretation of Scripture by a rabbinic sage.

Mishnah a law code, organized by topics, *c.* 200 C.E.

mitzvah commandment, divine imperative; *mitzvoth* (pl.).

monotheism belief in one all-powerful God.

motzi blessing said over bread before eating a meal, "Blessed are you, Lord, our God, king of the universe, who brings forth bread from the earth."

Nisan the lunar month that corresponds to March–April.

Num. Numbers.

Oral Torah the tradition revealed by God to Moses at Sinai and transmitted in a chain of oral, memorized traditions.

Passover the festival that commemorates the exodus of the children of Israel from Egyptian bondage; the "season of our freedom."

Pentecost the festival of weeks, celebrating the giving of the Torah at Mount Sinai by God to Moses; falls fifty days after Passover. Hebrew, Shabuot.

Pesiqta de Rab Kahana Rabbinic commentary on verses of Scripture read on special Sabbaths through the lunar year.

Pessah *see* Passover.

Pharisees Jewish sect in Second Temple times that practiced cultic cleanness not only in the temple, where it was required, but in meals at home, where it was not; and that emphasized strict Sabbath observance.

Prov. Proverbs.

Ps. Psalms.

Karaism medieval sect that rejected the rabbinic authority that was based on the belief in an oral tradition along with Scripture, and held that only the written part of the Torah was revealed by God to Moses at Sinai.

Rosh Hashanah New Year, first day of the lunar month of Tishré, in September–October.

Sabbateanism belief that Sabbatai Zevi was the Messiah, and that the Messiah would violate the laws of the Torah.

Sabbath day of rest on the seventh day of creation; on it God sanctified creation and rested; celebrates creation and the liberation of the Israelites from Egyptian bondage.

Sam. Samuel.

sanctified set apart as holy, for the service of God.

Seder order; Passover rite.

Sephardi a Jew whose ancestors originated in Spain or Portugal, generally expelled in 1492 from Spain; 1497 from Portugal, and settled in Italy and in the Ottoman Empire, in Turkey and Greece; preserved medieval Spanish as an ethnic language, called Ladino.

Shabbat Sabbath; tractate of the Mishnah.

Shabuot festival of weeks; Pentecost.

Shema "Hear O Israel," the first word of the proclamation of the monotheist creed.

Sifra rabbinic commentary to Leviticus.

Sifré to Numbers, Sifré to Deuteronomy rabbinic commentaries to the books of Numbers and Deuteronomy.

Sinai the mountain on which God revealed the Torah to Moses.

Sotah the wife accused of adultery and subjected to the ordeal described in Numbers 5, also a tractate of the Mishnah.

sukkot see huts.

taanit fast, a tractate of the Mishnah.

Tabernacles see huts.

Talmud a commentary to the Mishnah produced by the rabbinic sages from the first to the sixth centuries C.E. There are two Talmuds, the Bavli and the Yerushalmi.

Teleology, teleological theory of the purpose and goal of things.

Tishré the lunar month that coincides with the solar months of September–October.

Torah (1) instruction by God, particularly (2) the Pentateuch or Five Books of Moses, or (3) Scripture, or (4) rabbinic instruction based on oral tradition.

Tosefta a collection of laws that complement the Mishnah, *c.* 300 C.E.

Weeks *see* Shabuot / Pentecost.

Weltanschauung worldview, ethos.

Written Torah the Hebrew Scriptures, a.k.a. the Old Testament, in distinction from the oral Torah, the oral tradition revealed by God to Moses at Sinai.

Y. Yerushalmi, Talmud of the Land of Israel, produced in Galilee in *c.* 400 C.E.

Yom Kippur Day of Atonement, tenth day of the lunar month of Tishré.

Yoma The Day, referring to the Day of Atonement, a tractate of the Mishnah.

Yomim Noraim the Days of Awe, the penitential season from Rosh Hashanah to Yom Kippur.

Zionism political movement founded in 1897 that aimed to create a Jewish national homeland and a Jewish state in the Land of Israel, a.k.a. Palestine; achieved international recognition in 1917 with the Balfour Declaration and accomplished its purpose with the creation of the State of Israel in 1948.

BIBLIOGRAPHY

Avery-Peck, Alan J., and Neusner, Jacob (2003) *The Dictionary of Judaism*. London and New York: Routledge.

Avery-Peck, Alan J., Neusner, Jacob, and Scott Green, William (eds) (2005) *Encyclopaedia of Judaism*, 4 vols, 2nd edn. Leiden and Boston, Mass.: E. J. Brill.

Cohn-Sherbok, Dan (2003) *Judaism: History, Belief and Practice*. London: Routledge.

De Lange, N. R. M. (2003) *Judaism*, 2nd edn. Oxford: Oxford University Press.

Epstein, I. (1945) *Judaism*. London: Epworth Press.

Friedlander, Gerald (trans.) (1965) *Pirke de Rabbi Eliezer*. London: Sepher Hermon Press.

Goldin, Judah (trans.) (1955) *The Grace After Meals*. New York: The Jewish Theological Seminary of America.

Guttmann, Julius (1964) *Philosophies of Judaism: The History of Jewish Philosophy from Biblical Times to Franz Rosenzweig*, trans. by David Silverman. New York: Holt, Rinehart & Winston.

Hadas, Gershon (ed.) (1966) *Weekday Prayerbook*. New York: The Rabbinical Assembly.

Harlow, Jules (ed.) (1965) *Rabbi's Manual*. New York: The Rabbinical Assembly.

——(ed. and trans.) (1972) *The Mahzor*. New York: The Rabbinical Assembly.

Heinemann, Isaak (1960) "Judah Halevi, Kuzari," in *Three Jewish Philosophers*, ed. Isaak Heinemann, Alexander Altmann, and Hans Lewy. Philadelphia, Pa.: Jewish Publication Society.

Hertzberg, Arthur (1971) "Conservative Judaism," *Encyclopaedia Judaica*, Vol. V. Jerusalem: Keter, pp. 901–6.

Heschel, Abraham J. (1971) "The Mystical Elements of Judaism," in Louis Finkelstein (ed.) *The Jews: Their History, Culture, and Religion*. New York: Harper & Row.

Jacobs, Louis (1971) "Basic Ideas of Hasidism," *Encyclopaedia Judaica*, Vol. VII. Jerusalem: Keter, p. 1404.

——(1995) *The Jewish Religion: A Companion*. Oxford: Oxford University Press.

Katzburg, Nathaniel, and Wurzburger, Walter S. (1971) "Orthodoxy," *Encyclopaedia Judaica*, Vol. XII. Jerusalem: Keter, pp. 1486–93.

Kraemer, David Charles (1995) *Responses to Suffering in Classical Rabbinic Literature*. New York: Oxford University Press.

Levine, Baruch A. (2005) "Assyrian Ideology and Israelite Monotheism," *Iraq*, 67: 411–27.

Neusner, Jacob (1987a) *Death and Birth of Judaism. The Impact of Christianity, Secularism, and the Holocaust on Jewish Faith*. New York: Basic Books.

——(1987b) *Self-Fulfilling Prophecy: Exile and Return in the History of Judaism*. Boston, Mass.: Beacon Press.

——(1994) *Rabbinic Judaism. The Documentary History of the Formative Age*. Bethesda, Md.: CDL Press.

——(2003) *The Way of Torah. An Introduction to Judaism*, 7th edn. Belmont: Wadsworth / Thompson International.

Petuchowski, Jakob J. (1971) "Reform Judaism," *Encyclopaedia Judaica*, Vol. XIV. Jerusalem: Keter, pp. 23–8.

Rosen, D. (2003) *Understanding Judaism.* Edinburgh: Dunedin Academic Press.

Rubenstein, Richard L. (1966) *After Auschwitz: Radical Theology and Contemporary Judaism.* Indianapolis, Ind.: Bobbs-Merrill.

Samuel, Maurice (trans.) (1942) *Haggadah of Passover.* New York: Hebrew Publishing Co.

Schachter, Lifsa (1986) "Reflections on the Brit Mila Ceremony," *Conservative Judaism*, 38: 38–41.

Shapira, Anita (1974) *Berl: The Biography of a Socialist Zionist. Berl Katznelson 1887–1944.* Cambridge: Cambridge University Press.

Solomon, N. (2000) *Judaism: A Very Short Introduction.* Oxford: Oxford University Press.

Unterman, A. (1996) *Jews: Their Religious Beliefs and Practices*, 2nd edn. Brighton: Sussex Academic Press.

Wurzburger, Walter (1971) "Orthodox Judaism," *Encyclopaedia Judaica.* Jerusalem: Keter.

INDEX

Islam: The Basics
Colin Turner

With nearly 1500 rich years of history and culture to its name, Islam is one of the world's great faiths and, in modern times, the subject of increasingly passionate debate by believers and non-believers alike. *Islam: The Basics* is a concise and timely introduction to all aspects of Muslim belief and practice. Topics covered include:

- The Koran and its teachings
- The life of the Prophet Muhammad
- Women in Islam
- Sufism and Shi'ism
- Islam and the modern world
- Non-Muslim approaches to Islam

Complete with a glossary of terms, pointers to further reading and a chronology of key dates, *Islam: The Basics* provides an invaluable overview of the history and the contemporary relevance of this always fascinating and important subject.

0-415-34106-X

Available at all good bookshops
For ordering and further information please visit
www.routledge.com

Religion: The Basics
Malroy Nye

How does religion fit in with life in the modern world? Do you have to 'believe' to be a part of one?

From televangelism in the American South to the wearing of the hijab in Britain and Egypt; from the rise of paganism to the aftermath of 9/11, this accessible guide looks at the ways in which religion interacts with the everyday world in which we live. It is a comprehensive introduction to the world of religion, and covers aspects including:

- Religion and culture
- How power operates in religion
- Gender issues
- The role of belief, rituals and religious texts
- Religion in the contemporary world

Religion: The Basics offers an invaluable and up-to-date overview for anyone wanting to find out more about this fascinating subject.

"Finally, a book written for the general reader that communicates clearly and authoritatively the many advances that have taken place in the academic study of religion over the past generation."
Russell T McCutcheon, *University of Alabama*

0-415-26379-4

Available at all good bookshops
For ordering and further information please visit
www.routledge.com